THE REAL READER'

Slightly Foxed

'String is my Foible'

NO.76 WINTER 2022

Editors: Gail Pirkis & Hazel Wood
Editorial & submissions: Anna Kirk
Marketing & publicity: Steph Allen, Jennie Harrison Bunning & Hattie Summers
Subscriptions, orders & bookshops: Jess Dalby

Cover illustration: John Broadley, *Time at the Fox Inn*

Born in Huddersfield, John Broadley now lives and works in London. His highly detailed illustrations, characterized by rich texture and limited colour palettes, feature across a range of sectors, from food and drink to magazines and, more recently, children's books. Since 2012 he has been the in-house illustrator at Quo Vadis restaurant in Soho where his illustrations adorn the menus and interiors. Other clients include Fortnum & Mason, Berry Bros., Liberty, the *New Yorker*, the *Spectator*, the *New York Review of Books* and the *New York Times*. The book *While You're Sleeping* (Pavilion) was listed for several prizes and won a *New York Times* Best Illustrated Children's Book Award in 2021.

Design by Octavius Murray
Layout by Andrew Evans
Colophon and tailpiece by David Eccles

© The contributors 2022

Published by Slightly Foxed Limited
53 Hoxton Square
London N1 6PB

tel 020 7033 0258
email office@foxedquarterly.com
www.foxedquarterly.com

Slightly Foxed is published quarterly in early March, June, September and December

Annual subscription rates (4 issues)
UK and Ireland £48; Overseas £56

Single copies of this issue can be bought for £12.50 (UK) or £14.50 (Overseas)

All back issues in printed form are also available

ISBN 978-1-910898-74-1

ISSN 1742-5794

Printed and bound by Smith Settle, Yeadon, West Yorkshire

Contents

Contents

Clare Curtis

From the Editors

This issue of *Slightly Foxed* comes with our very best wishes to you all from all of us here for Christmas and the coming year. However there's no escaping the fact that these are anxious times, and we were touched by a reader in Australia who wrote to us recently: 'I can only say, to all the *Slightly Foxed* team, that you are a saviour. *Slightly Foxed* has kept me in touch, kept me sane, made me relish the humour, the warmth, the quirky charm of the English way of doing things.' Wherever you are in the world, we hope you feel the same.

'The English way of doing things' was certainly put to the test in 1956 when the late Sir Laurence Olivier made the ill-judged decision to direct and act in a film with Marilyn Monroe. The title was *The Prince and the Showgirl*, based on a play by Terence Rattigan. It was filmed at Pinewood Studios and from the moment Marilyn stepped off the plane, accompanied by her new husband Arthur Miller, her drama coach Paula Strasberg of the New York Actors Studio, and the rest of her American entourage, it was a disaster.

As it happened, young Colin Clark – son of Lord Clark of *Civilisation* – had used his contacts to get himself a job on set as a general dogsbody, and happily for us he kept a diary. *The Prince, the Showgirl and Me*, our Winter Slightly Foxed Edition (see p.13), is a sharp-eyed and hilarious account of the upstaging of poor Sir Laurence, the very embodiment of English professionalism, by an actress who rarely turned up on time and couldn't remember her lines but still magically outshone him on screen.

Another book to soothe the nerves and raise the spirits is this season's Plain Foxed Edition, *The Young Ardizzone*, a charming account

 by the author and illustrator Edward Ardizzone of his Edwardian childhood, much of it spent at the Suffolk home of his maternal grandmother in the company of his cheerful young unmarried uncles and characterful great-aunts. The story opens in 1905 when his mother brought her three small children to England from Haiphong where their father was a telegraph engineer. Like many colonial children, they didn't see her again for three years, and then only occasionally, once with a surprise new brother and sister in tow. It's a lovely book, written with the same gentle humour that distinguishes Ardizzone's affectionate illustrations, a must for fans and a perfect Christmas present for anyone who hasn't yet discovered him.

GAIL PIRKIS & HAZEL WOOD

The Slightly Foxed Podcast

A new episode of our podcast is available on the 15th of April, July, October and January. To listen, visit www.foxedquarterly.com/pod or search for Slightly Foxed on Audioboom, Apple Podcasts or your podcast app.

Subscriber Benefits

Slightly Foxed can obtain any books reviewed in this issue, whether new or second-hand. To enquire about a book, access the digital edition of *Slightly Foxed* or view a list of membership benefits, visit www.foxedquarterly.com/ members or contact the office: 020 7033 0258/office@foxedquarterly.com.

'String is my foible'

FELICITY JAMES

A tarnished silver teapot. A tin of buttons, their parent garments long decayed. A bundle of yellowing letters, in my mother's hand. Look: here she is, smiling in her nurse's uniform in the photograph that used to sit upon the mantelpiece. But now she's propped against moving boxes, still not unpacked. These are a few of the reasons why I cannot sit in my own front room, although there are more.

It's no use turning to Marie Kondo in this sort of situation; what I recommend is Elizabeth Gaskell. The narrator of *Cranford* (1851–3) knows all about hoarding. 'String is my foible. My pockets get full of little hanks of it, picked up and twisted together, ready for uses that never come.' And elastic bands – or, as *Cranford* puts it, India-rubber rings. Oh, don't talk about India-rubber rings! 'I have one which is not new,' our narrator tells us, 'one that I picked up off the floor, nearly six years ago. I have really tried to use it: but my heart failed me, and I could not commit the extravagance.'

Hoarding string might seem a perverse way to come at the charm of *Cranford*, Elizabeth Gaskell's much loved but somewhat under-valued series of stories from the early 1850s. But it is a telling image. *Cranford* is all about how we cling to the past, for good or ill: it is a novel about the pleasures, and pain, of nostalgia – the hank of string we cling to, lest we unravel altogether.

Ostensibly, *Cranford* is a gently comic novel of English village life:

Elizabeth Gaskell, *Cranford* (1853) · Penguin · Hb · 304pp · £14.99 · ISBN 9780141442549. There is also a fine biography by Jenny Uglow: *Elizabeth Gaskell* (1999) · Faber · Pb · 704pp · £14.99 · ISBN 9780571203598.

Elizabeth Gaskell by George Richmond
© National Portrait Gallery

old maids, tea-trays, curtained drawing-rooms. It takes the form of a series of recollections of Gaskell's own youth in Knutsford, where she spent her childhood in the 1810s, a railway ride away from Manchester. Knutsford retains something of its rural quaintness even now, especially the churchyard of the Dissenting chapel where Gaskell is buried, but it has had an infusion of football money. The streets are cluttered with expensive cars and the houses gleam with wealth in a way which would have been *so* distasteful to the spinsters of Cranford. The elderly women who live there are all adept at the art of 'elegant economy', trimming their candles watchfully, mending, making do. Not, you understand, out of necessity, but purely a question of choice and good breeding: spending money being 'always "vulgar and ostentatious"'. This is a world carefully buttressed with old-fashioned silver, with bread and butter sliced wafer-thin, with jealously preserved distinctions of rank and breeding.

In this little rural kingdom we seem to be very far from the big social and industrial tribulations of Gaskell's other novels, the class battles of *Mary Barton* or the historical sweep of *Sylvia's Lovers*. The dramas here are all local. Betty Barker's cow – of wonderful intelligence, and greatly superior milk – tumbles into a lime-pit and has to have a flannel waistcoat made to keep her from the cold. There is a report that a headless lady ghost has been seen in Darkness Lane. Mrs Forrester's lace, put to soak in milk, is swallowed by her cat. There is a dispute about the superiority of Dr Johnson over Charles Dickens. We see all this through the eyes of the young narrator, Mary, who goes to stay in Cranford with Miss Deborah and Miss Matty Jenkyns, elderly, straitened, but still highly conscious of their status as the Rector's daughters. Mary is affectionately, humorously tolerant of these Cranford eccentricities, and the spinsters' contrivances to preserve the remains of their gentility. That fine old lace, for example, 'the sole relic of better days', is rescued from its fate with the help of an emetic, administered to the cat in a teaspoon of currant-jelly: and now, as its owner proudly says at a tea-party, you 'would never guess that it had been in pussy's inside'.

But holding on to the past too tightly is also a curse. As the meandering recollections of Matty Jenkyns unfold in *Cranford* so too does our sense of sadness. Class distinctions, the source of so much comedy in the novel, are seen to have ruined her life, since she was forced to give up her suitor in early youth: 'they did not like Miss Matty to marry below her rank'. In *Cranford*, Gaskell shows how hard it is to outwit prejudice and fear, to overcome the pressure of the past and the dread of the judgement of others. And, especially, how hard it is to live up to the fearful ambition of a parent. Her style, as she unfolds Miss Matty's loss and secret pain, is close to the radical delicacy of Jane Austen. We are reminded of the revolutions in feeling of a Box Hill snub, or the pierced and silent heart of *Persuasion*, all conducted in the corner of a sitting-room, with the teapot standing by.

And just as in Austen's fiction, where the plots are shaped by the Napoleonic wars off-stage, in Cranford, we feel, even if we do not see directly, the upheavals of the nineteenth century: war, empire, rapacious industry. Gaskell, of course, knew these changes at first hand. She was as keen a social observer as Dickens, always alert to the cruelty visited on the poor and the powerless. Indeed, the first story about Cranford was written for Dickens's journal *Household Words* and appeared on 13 December 1851. Over the months that followed Gaskell was drawn into further recollections of her life and circle, which were finally published together as the book *Cranford* in 1853. It was slow going, because at the same time she was also writing her three-volume novel *Ruth*. Together the two works show us something of Gaskell's versatility and courage as a writer. *Ruth* is about the seduction of a young, orphaned seamstress by a feckless aristocratic son. Taken in and protected by a Dissenting clergyman and his sister, Ruth has her baby, and is passed off as a widow, only for her past to resurface and her façade of respectability to be destroyed. She finally emerges a heroine, albeit a dead one, since she becomes a selfless and beloved nurse who perishes in the service of others. The novel is a devastating condemnation of social hypocrisy.

What also stands out is Ruth's joy in her illegitimate baby. It was not simply the book's portrayal of the fallen woman, but the fallen woman's pleasure in motherhood, that shocked its early readers. Old friends and newspaper reviews alike expressed their 'deep regret' over Gaskell's choice of subject. Two members of one congregation burnt the book; 'a third has forbidden his wife to read it'; one young man piously declared he would not allow his *mother* to read it. The furore put Gaskell into a '*Ruth* fever', a real bout of sickness which laid her low, depressed and self-questioning. She emerged, however, to publish *Cranford* later the same year, which was read by relieved critics as a return to form, and a much more suitable and appropriate choice of subject. But the two are interlinked. The ladies of Cranford are haunted by just the same fears that torment Ruth: pain, poverty and death.

There is something else which unites the different aspects of Gaskell's fiction: at its heart is grief. For though her writing was in part prompted by her sense of social justice, it was also a consolation, a distraction and an occupation after the death in infancy of her little boy Willie, her second child, from scarlet fever. In April 1848 she wrote to a family friend:

> I have just been up to our room. There is a fire in it, and a smell of baking, and oddly enough the recollections of 3 years ago come over me strongly – when I used to sit up in the room so often in the evenings reading by the fire, and watching my darling darling Willie, who now sleeps sounder still in the dull, dreary church-yard at Warrington. That wound will never heal on this earth, although hardly anyone knows how it has changed me.

Her writing is always preoccupied with that wound. It pays close attention to the ebb and flow of recollection, of affection that exists only in memory, and it is especially interested in the currents of parental love. In *Ruth* we see mother and baby; in *Cranford* time stretches back and we see the old ladies as the cherished infants they once were, though they themselves have no one but their naughty pussy-cats to dote on. There is nothing so tender and elegiac in the whole of nineteenth-century literature as the scene where Miss Matty burns the family letters, lest they fall into the hands of strangers:

> There was in them a vivid and intense sense of the present time, which seemed so strong and full, as if it could never pass away, and as if the warm, living hearts that so expressed themselves could never die, and be as nothing to the sunny earth.

Here are the courtships of the 1770s, here are the announcements of new babies, now in the grave. How well Gaskell evokes the pathos that lies in the box of browning letters, the contrast between the longed-for child of the last century and the 'grey, withered, and wrinkled' woman she has become; the mother's hopes and the sad disappointments of the unfolding years.

This is, in truth, why I love the novel so much. Its loving portrayal of mothers becomes mixed up in my memory with my own mother. *Cranford* was a sacred book in our house, for it had tempted my mother into marriage. She was a nurse at the Manchester Royal Infirmary when my father came in with a detached retina. She had no time for courting: she was set upon becoming a Salvation Army missionary. Staunchly, she rebuffed him: but he held out the promise of a trip to Knutsford in his Morgan, simply to admire the haunts of Mrs Gaskell. What could be the harm?

I was the cosseted child of their old age, with whom she recollected the past and thought over how things might have been. It was only to me that she confided the poverty of her childhood, how hard she'd worked to smooth out her Lancashire accent and make herself into someone new. She had a special sympathy for all the small social snobberies of the ladies of Cranford, and their elegant economies. How secretively she guarded where she'd come from, before her glorious reinvention when she was accepted by the nursing school (the first ever without a school certificate – even now I feel a pang, part pride, part disloyalty, revealing that in print). How glad she was to own her own silver, when she'd begun by polishing that of other people; how shamelessly proud of my own school certificates. Yet how carefully she preserved things that might be used again, just in case dark times returned. And now, like the ladies of Cranford, I can't bear to part with her hoarded treasures, her old-fashioned silverware, my grief.

But if *Cranford* is about the pain of the past it is also about how to let it go. In burning those letters, Miss Matty lets in a beam of light. Though she will never have her love affair, she allows her maid to have her young man come calling: "'God forbid,' said she, in a low voice, "that I should grieve any young hearts.'" And when the bank fails, taking with it all her worldly goods, she enters on a new phase, selling tea and comfits from her own front room. She does nothing so ungenteel as turn a profit, but she's sustained by the love and friendship of those around her – and she ends by gaining something much more precious, a fragile happy ending in old age.

I open the door of the front room, just a crack. There is the teapot, blackened, baleful, looking as if it might have put on mourning itself. Perhaps I'll start with that. In honour of Miss Matty, I'll brew some orange pekoe. I might even tidy the letters and tie them with fresh string.

FELICITY JAMES grew up about twenty miles outside Manchester, and at least eighty years behind the times. She owes her existence to *Cranford*, and now repays the debt by researching Dissenting writers from the Lambs to Elizabeth Gaskell. You can also hear her in Episode 24 of our podcast, discussing the lives and letters of Charles and Mary Lamb.

Shall I Be Me?

DEREK PARKER

In the summer of 1953, briefly in London during the Coronation celebrations, I took myself to the Phoenix theatre (Upper Circle, 6s.) to see *The Sleeping Prince*, with the two glittering stars of the time, Laurence Olivier and his wife Vivien Leigh. Olivier had commissioned the piece especially for the season from the playwright Terence Rattigan, and the paper-thin plot had the Regent of Carpathia, in town for the 1911 Coronation, reluctantly mesmerized by a chorus girl. No play embellished by Olivier and Leigh could fail to captivate a popular audience, and this one had a good run – but for those with a more robust appetite it was really nothing more than a moderately tasty meringue.

Now fast forward to 1956, when Colin Clark, younger son of the art historian Kenneth Clark (later famous for his TV series *Civilisation*), left university determined to become a film director. With nepotism fluttering its obliging wings (Sir Kenneth was a friend of Sir Laurence) Colin managed to install himself as third assistant director on a film based on Rattigan's play, now retitled *The Prince and the Showgirl*. His position was as trivial as could be: that of a 'gofer' ('go for this', 'go for that'). But this was to be no run-of-the-mill film.

Olivier had fallen as heavily as any film fan for that sensation of the Western world, Marilyn Monroe, and she, flattered by an invitation from the greatest classical actor of the time, had agreed to come to England to star as Elsie, a showgirl, in a film to be made at Pinewood studios during her honeymoon with her most recent husband, the playwright Arthur Miller. One can perfectly understand

Olivier's confidence that the production would be a success, with Monroe straight from *The Seven Year Itch* and the notorious photograph of her standing astride that famous New York subway grating. He would direct the film himself – he could walk through his own part as the uptight Regent, and his international fame as a leading classical actor with an Oscar for film direction (*Hamlet*, 1948) would surely guarantee that Marilyn – who had a reputation for being uncontrollably difficult on set – would behave herself at Pinewood.

Happily, Colin Clark decided to keep a diary during the film's production, and in 1995, years after Monroe's death, it was published as *The Prince, the Showgirl and Me*, a title which suggested that it might be more than a dry record of this 'take' and that 'cut'. And so it is. On the page Colin seems at first naïve, brash and self-obsessed – but young as he was (24), after at first being roughed about a little by Olivier and the film crew, he became an objective and eager observer of life in and around the studios.

Marilyn soon identified herself as the infuriating personality advertised within her profession: late on set and usually unable to remember her lines or even what scene she was in. She was also accompanied by her drama coach, Paula Strasberg, the wife of Lee Strasberg, founder of the New York Actors Studio and the presiding god of 'Method' acting. Before and after every 'take' Marilyn had to report to Ms Strasberg and be sycophantically complimented and encouraged to be as wilful as might be. This drove the ultra-professional Olivier into paroxysms of ill-concealed rage. The fact that the 'rushes' showed a wooden performance from him while Marilyn lit up the screen with her every appearance did nothing to improve his temper – nor did the rebuke that the adorable Dame Sybil Thorndike actually delivered to him in front of the crew: 'Don't you realize what a strain this girl is under? She hasn't had your years of experience. She is in a strange country, trying to act in a strange part. Are you helping or bullying?'

Colin watched all this with mixed feelings. He was as appalled by

Marilyn's behaviour and amateurism as everyone else – but, also like everyone else, he saw that on-screen she was incandescent; she 'looked like an angel, smooth, glowing, eyes shining with joy, irresistible. We all fell in love there and then.' She, of course, hadn't noticed him, or so he thought – until one afternoon he was asked to pick up her script from her dressing-room while she was filming on set. But she wasn't on set: as he walked into the room,

Lighting up the screen

there stood MM, completely nude, with only a white towel round her head. I stopped dead. All I could see were beautiful white and pink curves. I must have gone as red a a beetroot. I couldn't even rush out, so just stood there and stared and stammered. MM gave me the most innocent smile. 'Oh Colin,' she said. 'And you an old Etonian!'

So she *had* noticed him – and somehow came to suspect, halfway through the production, that he was the only person at Pinewood who was 'on her side'. Paranoia was permanent, with some reason: she was surrounded by an unsympathetic director and impatient fellow actors, and off set by her coarse American 'minders', including a lawyer and an accountant. Her husband had made it clear he regarded his wife as his inferior in every way and had retreated to Manhattan. She relied on Colin more and more for sympathy and occasional giggles. Olivier, by now obsessed by her failure to match his own competence, was highly suspicious of their friendship – and puzzled by its nature – while the crew smirked and Marilyn's American 'protectors' worked hard to shield her from the young Englishman they increasingly believed to be obscurely dangerous.

Marilyn took a mischievous delight in irritating them and, as

Colin would later reveal in a short additional reminiscence, *My Week with Marilyn* (2000), one morning he was shocked to find her hiding under a blanket in the back of the car driven by her conniving police driver. 'I don't want to be Miss Monroe today,' she said; 'I just want to be me.' He found himself in the back seat, with the most desirable woman in the world cuddling up to him. Dizzily, he grasped the consequences of allowing her to become too close and proposed a sedate walk in Windsor Great Park. When that pleasure was exhausted, he recalled that his godfather happened to be the librarian at Windsor Castle, and Marilyn was shown around the private apartments. By the time they came to leave, a little crowd had gathered. Marilyn paused. 'Shall I be *her?*' she asked.

> Without waiting for an answer, she jumped up on a step and struck a pose. Her hip went out, her shoulders went back, her famous bosom was thrust forward. She pouted her lips and opened her eyes wide, and there suddenly was the image the whole world knew.

Later, they bought swimming costumes and bathed in the Thames. Marilyn's costume proved superfluous, as did reticence. 'You're the first person I've kissed who's younger than me,' she said, happily aware of his obvious confusion. When they drove back to the studios her furious lawyer threatened to sue Colin for 'enticement'. 'If you hurt one hair of his head,' Marilyn said, 'I'll be very, *very* upset. Understand?'

Later still, the relationship became more complicated. When she suspected she might be having a miscarriage, it was Colin to whom she appealed. Eluding her minders, he climbed a ladder to her locked bedroom and became her psychologist, analysing her marriages and her insecurities before falling innocently asleep in her arms.

If Colin's account is accurate, he was certainly a remarkable 24-year-old. But his diagnoses were right enough. And there was a little more clandestine psychology before the film was eventually completed, with Olivier continuing to treat Monroe as a stupid, infuriating, incompetent amateur. He could only acknowledge his wife's comment: 'He fell for her, and look where that got him.' In the end, the film finally complete, Marilyn's minders whisked her back to Hollywood and the set of the best film comedy ever made, *Some Like It Hot.*

Is Colin Clark's diary fact, or fact with a measure of fiction? Many of its pages echo evidence already freely available in earlier books, but what Clark manages to do is to show Monroe as the delightful child she could become when not in a dark mood, the too infrequent moments when, magically, she became perhaps the only great star whose fame equalled that of Garbo (who also, we might remember, had her problems). Doubters should sit through the indifferent film of Rattigan's comedy until they reach the scene in the Carpathian Embassy when she dances alone to the music of a barrel-organ outside in the street; one's short hairs rise amid the goosebumps. Clark gives us a believable portrait of the creature who could provoke that reaction. Fact or fiction? Well, after all, even in their diaries, not all writers are upon oath.

DEREK PARKER and his wife have returned to England after twenty years in Australia, and now live in Bognor Regis.

Uncle Quentin Revisited

TOM HODGKINSON

When I was 4 my parents took me to a junk shop in Richmond. They saw me examining a musty red hardback and asked if I'd like to buy it. It was *Five on Kirrin Island Again* (1947), the sixth in Enid Blyton's 'Famous Five' series, a 1950s edition with illustrations by Eileen Soper, though without a dust jacket.

This was the first proper novel I'd ever read. It took me a while to get my head around the fact that the separate chapters were not self-contained stories but part of a whole. I immediately became hooked and devoured the whole series, following the adventures of Julian, Dick, Anne, Georgina (George) and Timmy the dog over the following years.

As a 4-year-old I was absolutely terrified by the book's central character, Uncle Quentin. I remember hating him and all he stood for – an obsession with work, a hostility to children and a startling lack of fun genes. He found Julian, Dick, Anne and George really annoying and locked himself in his study. He shouted at them. He let his wife, Fanny, and the cook, Joanna, do all the domestic work. He was one of the most unsympathetic adults I'd so far encountered.

Eileen Soper

Enid Blyton, *Five on Kirrin Island Again* (1947): Hodder · Pb · 208pp · £6.99 · ISBN 9780340681114. The other titles in the series are available in paperback from Hodder individually or as a box set.

However I recently reread *Five on Kirrin Island Again* and, in the intervening fifty years, I find that Uncle Quentin has turned into a completely different character, one with whom I identify and hugely admire. Now he appears to me as a free spirit, very brave, something of a genius and also liberal to the point of being a proto-hippie.

For one thing, I now get his irritation with children and the noise they make. For years, when writing books and when my children were small, I became Uncle Quentin: obsessed by my own importance and excessively grumpy if disturbed. It's hard enough to motivate yourself to work with no boss and no external schedule. You can really do without the extra distraction of childish voices raised in play.

And Quentin had good reason to be grumpy: a detail that completely escaped me first time round was that he and Aunt Fanny had money worries. In fact, in the first book of the twenty-one-book series, *Five on a Treasure Island* (1942), Enid Blyton explains that a desperate need for cash is the reason they take in his brother's children – Julian, Dick and Anne – for the holidays. It's not a favour. These problems attend the freelance life. I had to do something similar when we were skint a while ago: we let out our eldest son's bedroom to Airbnb guests at weekends. So Quentin, I feel your pain. I'd guess that the mere presence of the three children – at least earlier in the series – acts as a constant reminder of your impecunious state. No wonder you find them annoying.

It's also striking how young and good-looking Quentin is, at least as represented by Eileen Soper. He has a square jaw and a mass of black hair. The only weird thing is that Soper puts everyone in outsize boxy jackets, so that Quentin faintly resembles the singer David Byrne in the 1980s film *Stop Making Sense*.

Now let's look at Quentin's work. This is clearly a fascinating area. With those brains – that's his USP, isn't it? As everyone says, 'He's remarkably clever' – he could have joined the Foreign Office or made a fortune in the City. Instead he has chosen to become a freelance inventor. He is an outlaw, he has morals, he has shunned the rat race,

he has refused to submit to the indignities of conventional employment, and he must suffer the financial insecurity that results. In other
words, he is a hero.

In *Five on Kirrin Island Again*, Blyton holds Uncle Quentin and
his life choices up as a model to the children. I was surprised to find
that Julian – who I'd always seen as the squarest of the five, the sort
of chap who when grown up would get a job in marine insurance
and watch the rugby at weekends – is in fact inspired to follow an
unconventional path by Quentin's example: 'I wouldn't mind being
a scientist myself,' he says to the others. 'I want to be something
really worthwhile when I grow up – I'm not just going into some-
body's office. I'm going to be on my own.' Well said, Jools!

The story opens when the four children arrive at Kirrin Cottage
for the holidays to find that Quentin has taken over nearby Kirrin
Island for his experiments, even though it technically belongs to his
daughter George; she finds this takeover incredibly annoying and
Aunt Fanny has to explain that it's for the best. She doesn't in fact
know the details of what Quentin is up to but, she says, 'I do know
it's terribly important – and I know, of course, that the last part of
the experiment has to be made in a place where there is deep water
all around. Don't ask me why – I don't know.'

Quentin's absence from Kirrin Cottage comes as something of a
relief to the nervous Anne, who confides to her brother: 'You know,
Dick, I'm really quite pleased that Uncle Quentin has gone to Kirrin
Island, even if it means we won't be able to go there much! I feel
much freer in the house when he's away. He's a very clever man and
he can be awfully nice – but I always feel a bit afraid of him.' Too
right, sister.

Now what is really remarkable in *Five on Kirrin Island Again* is the
visionary brilliance of Quentin's project, which is only revealed
towards the end of the book. The children decide to visit the island
one day, in the company of Aunt Fanny, to try to find out what he's
up to. Blyton tells us that he's constructed a glowing edifice: 'Rising

from the centre of the castle, probably from the castle yard, was a tall, thin tower, rather like a lighthouse.' Well, well. What on earth could that be?

The children poke about in the tower and then, eventually, run into Quentin, whereupon he flies into one of his terrifying rages. 'You've no business to come over here, and interfere with my work . . . How did you get into that tower? I locked it.' Anne is curious to find out what Quentin's up to: 'Uncle, you're not inventing a new atom bomb or anything, are you?' she asks courageously.

> Her uncle looked at her scornfully. 'I wouldn't waste my time inventing things that will be used to kill and maim people! No – I'm inventing something that will be of the greatest use to humanity. You wait and see!'

Thus we learn that to add to his other virtues, Quentin is morally principled.

A few days later, under cover of night, George rows over to the island and discovers a new secret passage. It leads to underground bunkers filled with mysterious wires that hum like thousands of bees in a hive. She finds Quentin in a cave, and he reveals the revolutionary nature of his work.

> 'I'll tell you what my experiments are for, George – they are to find a way of replacing all coal, coke and oil – an idea to give the world all the heat and power it wants, and to do away with mines and miners.'
>
> 'Good gracious!' said George. 'It would be one of the most wonderful things the world has ever known.'

It would indeed. Quentin's carbon-neutral system of generating power from the waves, a hydro-electric plant, would save lives and save the planet. Very Greta Thunberg for 1947, I'd say. And unlike Elon Musk or Jeff Bezos, he appears to have no desire to monetize his invention. As well as being fervently Green, he is also anti-capitalist:

'And I should *give* it to the whole world – it shall not be in the power of any one country, or collection of men. It shall be a gift to the whole of mankind – but, George, there are men who want my secret for themselves, so that they may make colossal fortunes out of it.'

These men are called Johnson and Peters and they're greedy capitalists who presumably work for some multinational. They have parachuted on to the island and have already caught and tied up poor Timmy! The action unfolds. George manages to outwit the two bad men. Timmy rescues Quentin's plans and delivers them back to the mainland via an underground passage. And George's bravery earns her a commendation from her dad:

'Honestly, George, you do behave as bravely as any boy. I'm proud of you.'

George thought that was the nicest thing her father had ever said to her.

My feminist mother interpreted this exchange and others like it as evidence of a sexist culture where boys were seen as superior to girls and owned virtues like bravery. Anne is always bursting into tears and it's assumed she is less intelligent than the boys: for example, when the Five find out that their neighbour is a journalist, Dick feels the need to explain the term to his sister: 'That's a man who writes for the newspapers, Anne.'

However, with a pair of twenty-first-century spectacles on, we can see that Quentin is in fact deeply forward-thinking and liberal: he respects George's wish to identify as a boy. And no one around her, I'd add, shows any signs of transphobia. Even the villains of the piece – to George's delight – get her assumed gender right. 'Good heavens! A boy!' says one of them when apprehended by George in the subterranean passage. (We can imagine George's Twitter handle: George Kirrin. Student. Dog lover. Pronouns: he/him.)

Towards the end of the book there is a great showdown between the villains and Quentin which achieves a Bond-like intensity. The bad guys, Johnson and Peters, attempt to do a deal with Quentin.

'If you will tell us what we want to know, and give us all your notes, we will set you free, give you whatever sum of money you ask us for, and disappear ourselves.'

'And if I still say I won't?' said George's father.

'Then I am afraid we shall blow up the whole of your machines and the tower – and possibly you will never be found again because you will be buried down here,' said the man, in a voice that was suddenly very hard.

Quentin refuses. In other words, he turns down unimaginable riches – even though he's skint – in order to save the planet. And the plan by the evil capitalist scumbags to make billions out of Quentin's invention – or destroy it – is foiled, thanks to the intervention of the Famous Five.

The finale finds Quentin smashing up his own tower in order to prevent the evil men from carrying out their plan to blow up the island. The police arrive to take Johnson and Peters away and Quentin allows himself an 'in your face' moment: 'Your little plan went wrong. My secret is still safe – and next year it will be given to the whole world!'

'Woof,' said Timmy.

TOM HODGKINSON is editor of the *Idler* magazine and author of several books including *How to be Idle* and *Business for Bohemians*. You can also hear him in Episode 39 of our podcast, discussing literary loafers through the ages.

Surprised by Joy

KRISTIAN DOYLE

In the obituaries that appeared in 2021 for the Polish writer Adam Zagajewski, his prose, I was saddened to see, hardly got a mention. I suppose this is common with poets: their poetry is seen as the real work, and everything else is a sideline, left-handed writing. This is, to be fair, often the case. But Zagajewski was genuinely ambidextrous, writing just as many books of prose as poetry, and just as seriously. It was essentially the same work, only in a different form.

Of his five prose books to have been translated into English, the last, *Slight Exaggeration*, is my favourite. It's hard to classify: a fragmentary mix of literary and cultural criticism, aphorisms, Central and Eastern European history, biography and, above all, autobiography – even if mostly oblique autobiography. Whatever it is, though, it's also the kind of book that could do with an introduction.

It begins, misleadingly, like a rarefied aesthete's diary. In the first entry, Zagajewski remembers the previous night's Shostakovich concert; the third begins, 'I'm reading about Gottfried Benn in *Poetry* magazine', and the fourth, 'I've been reading Karl Corino's thick biography of Robert Musil'. It's not exactly auspicious, and he goes on like this for a little while longer, referring to almost two dozen writers or composers in the first ten pages alone. Fortunately, this is just throat-clearing: the book hasn't yet found its raison d'être. It's when he alights on memories of a recent trip to Lviv, his birthplace, that *Slight Exaggeration* opens up. From that point on, what began

Adam Zagajewski, *Slight Exaggeration: An Essay* (2011: English edition 2017), is out of print but we can obtain second-hand copies.

merely as fleshed-out notes of concerts attended and books read becomes instead a work of profound retrospection, a wise and beautiful final accounting of what is, to my mind, a truly exemplary life.

For Zagajewski, Lviv will always be Lvov. It's a city with a complicated, unfortunate history – in the twentieth century alone, it changed hands five times. Now, it's Ukrainian, but at the time of Zagajewski's birth in 1945 it belonged to Poland. When he was only a few months old, though, it was given to the Soviet Union as part of the post-war reorganization of Europe, and most of the city's Polish population were expelled. Zagajewski and his family ended up in the drab industrial town of Gliwice in western Poland – a world away from the ancient splendour of Lvov.

As a result he never had a chance to know his birthplace other than as a tourist, but it was central to his work. Much of *Slight Exaggeration* reads, in fact, like a prose continuation of 'To Go to Lvov', the monumental opening poem of his first English-language collection, written over three decades earlier. In this elegy he charts the city's transformation from ancestral homeland into a place of imagination: the lost paradise in which his parents, his grandparents and many of the other exiles lived in their minds: '. . . go to Lvov', it ends, 'after all/ it exists, quiet and pure as/ a peach. It is everywhere.'

In *Slight Exaggeration*, he continues to be fascinated by the city's hold on his family, though now he sees through and around the myth. 'I think about Aunt Ania,' he writes early on, 'who never made peace with her new surroundings and even now, at ninety-something, remains a sceptical immigrant in her new town (new, some sixty years later!) . . . About my grandfather, how in his last years he . . . thought that by some miracle he'd gone back to his Lvov'. And about his father, for whom the city becomes a literal heaven: 'After he'd already started to lose his memory, he once told Mrs L, who looked after him, "You know, I'll be seeing my wife soon, I'm going to Lvov." My mother was no longer living.'

Zagajewski's own feelings are never quite settled. He occasionally tries to sound dispassionate, aloof: 'I didn't suffer, I was an observer, not an emigrant.' And when his friends give him presents linked to the city – 'old engravings, maps, yet another book on our lost paradise' – he'd like to 'set them straight, to explain that such things don't interest me'. And yet such things *do* interest him, and he does suffer: 'It's easy to satirize the perfect idyll that exiles find years later in their vanished homeland,' he writes later, 'but I never think of that lost city without pain. It pains me to know that I never lived there, the great vacuum of what never was, the childhood that should have been and wasn't . . . the loves I didn't meet, the familiarity with stones and trees, with streets I'll never know.'

But he also uses the city's symbolic power for his own ends, formulating a theory of suffering that is full of the true poet's self-serving naïvety. The displaced had lost much, he writes, but 'by way of the turbulence, the mystery they bore within them', they became artists. Unlike those 'who'd never been deported, who'd never had to abandon family graves, family homes, native landscapes', the displaced 'carry secrets, they bear a loss, an abyss, a longing within them . . . their lives contain great stockpiles of meaning'. And being born among them, he believes, marked him for life: 'I might never have taken up writing if not for [those] unhappy exiles.'

Later, he too became an exile. In the 1970s, as a vocal critic of Poland's communist government, his books were banned and he struggled to make a living. So in 1982, he and his partner, the actress Maja Wodecka, fled to Paris, where he lived for the next twenty years. Thus began a period of semi-itinerancy. Paris was never quite home: he was often away, at conferences, giving readings or lecturing. After the first English-language edition of his poems was published in 1985, he accepted an invitation to teach one semester a year at the University of Houston. For almost two decades he kept this up, each year leaving Paris in the winter and returning four months later.

In the fragments he gives us in *Slight Exaggeration* – reports not only from Paris and Houston, but also Krakow (where he returned to live in 2002), Chicago (where he taught after leaving Houston), Berlin, Bologna, Venice, Dresden and Athens, among others – he bears witness to a life that, after the turbulence and strife of its first half, has settled into a kind of cosmopolitan idyll.

But its allure has less to do with the places themselves than with the spirit Zagajewski brings to them. His partly inherited sense of displacement – what he calls his homelessness – gives him a kind of innocent orientation to his surroundings, lends a beautiful novelty to everything he sees. Wherever he is, he remains always the unjaded non-native, 'intoxicated with the world', as Miłosz said of his poetry.

'I also liked the smell of the Berlin metro,' he writes in one typical digression,

> which remains unchanged to this very day; I got to know other subways later, in London, Barcelona, Rome and other metropolises, but I've never encountered the precise, sober smell of the Berlin metro – like brown coal . . . a raw aroma, as if Germanic geological strata had been unearthed when the metro was constructed. Few thought to delight in this subterranean world – for most people, after all, it was chiefly a key component in so-called urban transportation . . . they didn't notice their extraordinary location, a place demanding veneration, a moment of reflection, meditation.

He is a great praiser, and he tries to take as his credo a line of Paul Claudel's: 'He who admires is never wrong.' In *Slight Exaggeration* he lovingly returns again and again to his pantheon of composers, artists and, above all, writers – Weil, Cioran, Czapski, Proust, Benn, Rilke, Miłosz, Montale, Elzenberg, Mandelstam – most of whom have been a presence in his work for decades. At this stage in his life, he is especially fond of 'those little books, portable volumes holding poems, aphorisms, observations, brief essays, diarists' notes' by some of the above, which serve as splendid companions on long strolls. 'Gatherings of great moments', he calls these prized pocketbooks.

A deep vein of spirituality runs through *Slight Exaggeration*. I can't think of another serious contemporary writer as liberal with the use of the word 'soul', for example. And those 'great moments', rather than being of merely aesthetic import, have for Zagajewski a significance that borders on the holy: 'Great moments,' he writes, 'instants of elation, of short-lived certainty, light, faith . . . these moments form the base, the foundation of everything.'

Still, his spirituality almost always remains grounded in the here-and-now. At one point he tries to go further: 'The author believes in the existence of a higher world,' he writes, in a slightly embarrassed and atypical third-person aside, but it's quickly undercut. He cannot bring this world into being within his daily life: 'At most a few pages in his books mark efforts, always failed, always faulty, to attain this higher realm.'

It is, in the end, a spiritual yearning destined to remain earth-bound – but happily. 'Mysticism for Beginners', he called one of his best-known poems, and as a label for his beliefs you could do a lot worse. Indeed, in *Slight Exaggeration*, he returns to this poem – it's one of his favourites – and the account he gives of its ironic inception seems to encourage this reading. 'Sometime in the mid-nineties,' he writes, 'in May, in a Tuscan village where impossibly swift swallows flitted through narrow streets, we ended up in a crowded café . . . and at the next table I saw a German tourist reading a little book [called] *Mysticism for Beginners*.' He found it 'a little silly, to tell the truth', this 'how-to book for spiritual searchers' – but then, he goes on,

I experienced an epiphany: poetry is mysticism for beginners. That German tourist travelling through Tuscany with his funny little book helped me to realize that poetry differs from religion in essential ways, that poetry stops at a certain moment, stifles its exaltation, doesn't enter the monastery, it remains in the world, among the swallows and the tourists, among palpable, visible things.

Not just poetry, but the poet, too. There's a beautifully plain-spoken passage late in the book in which Zagajewski lives out – to an uncanny degree – this very vision. It is, for me, the self-portrait by which he ought to be remembered: a man for whom, finally, the 'palpable, visible things' of this world were enough – were more than enough.

'A moment of happiness, inexplicable, while strolling along the Vistula', he writes:

> It was a warm afternoon and it began to rain. I had an umbrella with me, but I took refuge nonetheless in the gate of a house on Smocza Street . . . near the Church on the Rock, in whose crypt Czesław Miłosz now rests, and I stood there for some time, looking at the poplars and sniffing their branches' bitter scent, which I like so much and remember from my childhood in Gliwice. I wasn't in a hurry, I waited for the rain to stop and felt a joy whose only source, so it seems, was that the world existed, it was May, and a new generation of swifts, looking like their precursors' twins, were whistling shrilly.

KRISTIAN DOYLE is a writer who lives in Liverpool. *Prayers*, a non-fiction pamphlet, is forthcoming from Broken Sleep Books this December.

A Northern Survivor

PAMELA BEASANT

Iain Ashman

Nestled in the heart of Orkney's second largest town, on a main street uncoiling, as the Orcadian poet and writer George Mackay Brown described it, 'like a sailor's rope', Stromness Books & Prints has several claims to fame. It's the UK's most northerly independent bookshop, and it's 'Scotland's only drive-in bookshop', as claimed by Tam MacPhail, who ran the business for many years. (This claim is based on the fact that the main street is narrow enough for drivers to stop outside the shop, open the window, shout a request through the door and be served without leaving the car.)

Another claim to fame is its survival; no mean feat in a time of online shopping and a global pandemic. It's more than just a shop in a small town. For businesses to embed here, they have to become part of the community; they offer something that can't be ordered online or found in a mainstream outlet. What the bookshop offers is the accumulated and eclectic knowledge of the successive owners (only four) since the shop opened its doors in 1970. It's a kind of magical threshold, where you discover things you never imagined, and end up reading something obscure and wonderful, because it's there, or because the current owner Sheena recommends it.

And one of the most important things about the business is the way it is handed on. No adverts or interviews – it's a much more mysterious process. The bookshop has to be earned over time, and the new owner is chosen by the current one in a long, organic period

Stromness Books & Prints, 3 Graham Place, Stromness, Orkney KW16 3BY, tel. 01856 850565 of 'growing into it', which has nothing to do with experience or qualifications, but everything to do with what goes on inside the person's head, their passion for reading and how they come to fit the shape of the chair behind the counter.

The founder of the shop was Charles Senior, poet, who at first sold only second-hand books, including some rare and valuable anti-quarian volumes. Senior was a friend and confidant of George Mackay Brown. The two men met in Edinburgh when the latter was at Edinburgh University, part of the extraordinary group of poets and writers who haunted Milne's Bar in Rose Street. They corresponded weekly until Charles Senior moved to Stromness in 1968. He handed on the bookshop to his friend John Broom (whose name can still be seen above the door), a librarian, also an old friend of GMB's, who moved to the islands in the early Seventies and introduced a new range of little Pelican books. When John was offered the post of librarian in Stromness Library, he handed the business to Tam MacPhail, a sculptor originally from California, who had been work-ing in the bookshop since 1976. (Tam started selling maps along with the books and restored the original name of Stromness Books & Prints.) Finally, in 2014, Tam handed the business to Sheena Winter, who grew up in Edinburgh but has strong Orkney roots, and who had been working with him since 1998. Sheena has made it her own, although Tam appeared regularly until his death in 2020, and the shop is often still called simply 'Tam's' by locals.

That's the succession in a nutshell, but behind it is a bigger story, of course, to do with the four bookshop owners, their interwoven lives in the community, and the place itself.

Outwardly, central Stromness has changed little since its first beginnings. From the pierhead, the main street undulates for around five hundred metres until it reaches the Point of Ness overlooking Hoy Sound, with the little island of Graemsay in the foreground, and the Hoy hills looming behind; a benign and protective barrier against the restless Pentland Firth. It's the best view in Orkney.

In Stromness, the ferry to the Scottish mainland comes and goes daily, punctuating the days and the lives of the 1,800 inhabitants. The rumble of its engines can be felt right through the foundations of the stone houses, and it's comforting to feel it and know the ferry is in.

The town has always been a busy place, from the days of whaling and the Hudson's Bay Company in the nineteenth century, when Canada-bound ships put into Stromness for water and supplies and employed Orcadians as sailors or as trappers, traders and cartographers in the far north. And it's as busy as ever today. Alongside the traditional mix of fishermen, farmers, teachers and shopkeepers, the town is one of the most innovative centres of renewable energy in the world. It also has a cutting-edge creative community, and archaeologists who are attracted by Orkney's world-renowned Neolithic and Norse sites. Long-established businesses include Flett's the butcher, Argo's bakery (now housing the Post Office), the North End Garage, Sinclair's fishing tackle and gift shop, Wishart's hardware shop, the Waterfront Gallery, the Quernstone, Sinclair's Office Supplies and Julia's café. And new businesses have sprung up more recently, offering gallery space, diving equipment, toys, gifts, groceries and takeaway food. You can find just about anything in Stromness, if you know where to look.

In amongst it all, the bookshop has not only survived but thrived. And it's done this in a tiny space, with no running water and no toilet. Two customers fit in the shop comfortably, three's a bit of a squash. There are books from floor to ceiling, and the clientele varies from tourists looking for maps, guides or a good holiday read, to locals who are fiercely loyal and resist the call of Amazon. George Mackay Brown, who lived nearby in an ex-council house, was a close friend of Tam and his wife, the Swedish-born photographer and artist Gunnie Moberg.

George and Gunnie produced many books, including a few they collaborated on, and all can be found in the bookshop. (The beautiful book *Orkney: Pictures and Poems* came about when Gunnie fed images to George, which he propped up in front of him and responded to. Gunnie had initially asked for captions, but he produced a significant series of poems.) There are also books about the extraordinary history of Orkney, its unique bird and wildlife, folklore and mythology; books on philosophy, religion and politics; and there's a whole children's section and a wonderful poetry and contemporary literature collection, including every interesting writer you can think of and many volumes and limited editions by local authors.

A canny and discreet expansion of the bookshop can be found in the Pier Arts Centre, just a couple of hundred metres north up the street. The gallery is a tale in itself, housing a permanent collection by St Ives artists such as Barbara Hepworth and Ben Nicholson, gifted by Margaret Gardiner in the 1970s. The collection has grown over the years so that it's now one of the most significant in the UK, and there are temporary exhibitions by some of the most exciting and innovative contemporary artists. In the foyer, with the cards and gifts, is an impressive collection of art books under the auspices of Stromness Books & Prints.

The business was built by Tam over many years, and in the shop his presence can still be felt. He was an extraordinary man – a gifted artist (although the bookshop took up most of his time) with an intense, quietly restless mental energy. Some were a bit scared of him; he could be unreadable, and his sense of humour was very particular. He had a quirky, creative turn of mind. But Tam was also a man of huge kindness and generosity who inspired great loyalty; he was utterly devoted to his wife Gunnie and their four sons and he forged many close friendships locally. When Gunnie died in 2007 he was never quite the same again, and when his own health began to fail, there was a sense of disbelief that old age and infirmity could be applied to Tam; he had always seemed ageless and agile, mentally and physically. There was something other about him; a kind of magic. When he died, during the lockdown in 2020, there was a huge outpouring of sadness. Many people lined the streets when his wicker coffin was driven past the bookshop, where it paused for people to raise a glass and say their goodbyes. The sense of the significance of the loss was shared by all.

In the recently built Warehouse Buildings at the Pierhead, housing Stromness Library, an enormous portrait of Tam, by local artist and friend Calum Morrison, dominates the main staircase. He's painted behind the counter of the shop, with books gloriously in flight all around his head, Chagall-like. At the still centre, Tam looks out with a characteristically enigmatic expression. It provokes a jolt of sadness now that he's gone – but also recognition of how truthfully the painting catches him.

Over the past few years, Sheena has discreetly brought the business into the twenty-first century. Until recently, the bookshop didn't accept card payments, only cash or cheques. (And Tam didn't believe in giving a penny change; locals learned not to ask for it.) Sheena now stocks national book tokens, but you can still buy exclusive bookshop ones, hand-made from old cards, with the amount written in silver or gold pen with an added 'valid forever'. (If you don't spend it all, Sheena crosses out the amount and writes what's left underneath. Brilliant.) She has kept the Tam-infused feel and integrity of the space, but there's an ever-changing, dynamic stock, more choice on how to pay, and she will source obscure or out-of-print books online, order them in and charge only what she paid. Sheena simply loves books, and she wants people to be able to get them in whatever way possible. And this is the key to the bookshop's success. It's never been run as a business first. From a tiny space, in a small town in the far north, it's been run with community-embedded, outward-looking intelligence, with multi-layered curiosity about the world and its wonderful literature, and, above all, it's been run with love. It's a survivor, and, as Larkin said, 'what will survive of us is love'.

PAMELA BEASANT is a poet, author and playwright. Originally from Glasgow, she has been living in Stromness, Orkney, for many years.

Double Trouble

ANTHONY GARDNER

Duelling was a daily feature of my prep-school life. Our swords were wooden rulers; chipped and battered desks served as castle battlements. Modern warfare held a fascination too, but when it came to single combat and displays of derring-do, our hearts belonged to an earlier age – and no book captured it better than Anthony Hope's 1894 novel *The Prisoner of Zenda*.

The title was instantly intriguing. Who was the prisoner? Why was he or she incarcerated? And where on earth was Zenda?

The answer to the last question was, of course, Ruritania: a 'highly interesting and important kingdom' which had played 'no small part' in European history. Hope – an extremely clever man who took a First in Greats at Oxford and gave up a promising legal career to write – placed it cannily somewhere to the east of Germany, where the average Briton's grasp of geography starts to become vague. Alien but not unrecognizable, it came with dramatic scenery, the glamour of a monarchy upheld by shakoed hussars, and few of the mundane trappings of industrialization: though it possessed a railway, there were plenty of situations in which a heart-in-the-mouth gallop on a foam-flecked steed provided the only way out.

Hope, who had a gift for names, chose a very peculiar one for his hero: Rudolph Rassendyll. It suggests that, despite his thoroughly English demeanour, there is a touch of the foreigner about him – which, indeed, there is. The opening pages tell us that in 1733 a noble

Anthony Hope, *The Prisoner of Zenda* (1894)
Macmillan · Hb · 208pp · £9.99 · ISBN 9781509834587

ancestress had an affair with the crown prince of Ruritania, and that every few generations a Rassendyll appears who shares the prince's sharp nose and bright red hair. Rudolph, crucially, is one of these.

Rudolph acts as the book's narrator, and the languid, Wildean tone in which he begins his story is a delight. 'Why in the world should I do anything?' he demands when his sister-in-law suggests that he find useful employment. 'I have an income nearly sufficient for my wants . . . I enjoy an admirable social position . . . Behold, it is enough!' If anyone is to blame for his idleness, it is his parents, who 'had no business to leave me two thousand pounds a year and a roving disposition'.

In its unpromising hero *The Prisoner of Zenda* anticipates two other classic adventure stories, *The Scarlet Pimpernel* and *The Riddle of the Sands*. Like Baroness Orczy's Sir Percy Blakeney and Erskine Childers' Carruthers, Rudolph is far more capable than he initially appears. He is a good swordsman, a fine shot, an excellent linguist – and, as we are about to discover, infinitely resourceful.

When he learns that Ruritania's new king is about to be crowned, Rudolph decides to visit the country for the occasion. Walking in the woods just after his arrival, he meets two men who stare at him in astonishment. One is an old soldier, Colonel Sapt; the other is a young courtier, Fritz von Tarlenheim. The reason for their surprise becomes clear when a third man appears: the king, who looks so like Rudolph as to be virtually indistinguishable.

The king takes the discovery in good part and invites Rudolph to dine with him at the hunting lodge where he is spending the night before his coronation. But the lodge belongs to his half-brother – known as Black Michael because of his very different hair colour – who wants the throne for himself. One of his men serves the king a bottle of wine so heavily drugged that he cannot be roused the next morning.

Sapt and Fritz explain the danger of the situation to Rudolph. If the king fails to appear for his coronation, Black Michael – who has a strong following among the poorer classes – will try to seize power. There is only one thing for it: Rudolph must take the king's place.

Of all God's gifts to writers, the fact that two very different people can look the same is one of the greatest. The Roman playwright Plautus rejoiced in it, as of course did Shakespeare, who borrowed the plot of Plautus' *Menaechmi* for *The Comedy of Errors*. Having a socially inferior character mistaken for a monarch makes the mix richer still – something Hope may have recognized in Mark Twain's 1881 novel *The Prince and the Pauper*.

With a political plot, the normal scenario is for the villains to try to replace the legitimate ruler with a doppelgänger whom they can manipulate. (This is the plot of the captivating Hollywood comedy *Dave*, in which Kevin Kline plays a well-meaning everyman catapulted into the White House.) Hope, however, chooses the opposite approach: in this case the substitution is for the ruler's own good.

Rudolph agrees to go along with the plan on condition that he can slip back to England once the coronation is over. Coached by Sapt, he fools everyone – including the king's intended wife, the beautiful Princess Flavia – and is duly crowned in the capital's magnificent cathedral. But on returning to the hunting lodge, he and his two allies make a terrible discovery: the king has been kidnapped by Black Michael's men and taken to the formidable Castle of Zenda.

Anthony Hope, a master of plot, thus creates a classic impasse. Rudolph cannot expose Black Michael without confessing that he has taken the coronation oath as an impostor. Equally, Black Michael cannot expose Rudolph without admitting that he has kidnapped the king. The king's life is safe for the time being because there is no point in killing him if Rudolph is there to occupy the throne instead; but Rudolph cannot attempt a rescue without putting both their lives at risk.

To drive events forward, Hope turns to Princess Flavia. Rudolph has been instantly smitten by her, and Sapt and Fritz advise him that publicly courting her will give a vital boost to the king's popularity.

But Rudolph is all too aware of the temptation before him: abandoning the king would allow him to keep Flavia – and by extension the throne – for himself. As a man of honour, he must carry out a rescue before that temptation becomes too great.

Flavia, it must be admitted, is an entirely one-dimensional character. So too is Black Michael, who remains largely in the background, leaving his dirty work to a band of gentlemen known as the Six. Chief among these is Rupert of Hentzau.

Young and handsome, Rupert is a thoroughgoing cad, loyal only to himself, with a reputation as a seducer; offering Rudolph a handshake, he treacherously stabs him with a hidden dagger. Yet there is something about him that even Rudolph finds irresistible: what Edmund Rostand would define in *Cyrano de Bergerac* as 'panache'. Rupert lives life to the full and literally laughs in the face of danger: 'For my part,' Rudolph reflects, 'if a man must needs be a knave, I would have him a debonair knave . . . It makes your sin no worse, as I conceive, to do it à la mode and stylishly.' It's fascinating to see this villain upstaging all the respectable characters, including the hero; tellingly, Rupert rather than Rudolph was the role taken by Douglas Fairbanks Jnr in the 1937 film version.

Rupert of Hentzau,
by Michael Godfrey

The Prisoner of Zenda culminates, inevitably, with Rudolph's attempt to rescue the king from Black Michael's stronghold. It would be unfair to reveal the many twists and turns of the showdown; suffice it to say that there is no shortage of swordfights on parapets and plunges into the moat. One can easily imagine the delight Hope must have taken in planning the layout of the castle and deploying his characters across it.

After the last pistol has been fired and the last sword sheathed, there remains the question of Princess Flavia, who feels far more attracted to the disguised Rudolph than she ever did to the king. One-dimensional she may be, but Hope imbues their relationship with unexpected pathos as they face an agonizing choice between love and duty. At the same time, he lays the ground neatly for the novel's equally exciting sequel, called – in confirmation of the villain's status – *Rupert of Hentzau* (1898).

The Prisoner of Zenda was an instant success, inspiring a whole genre of books that came to be known as 'Ruritanian romances'. Edgar Rice Burroughs wrote one (*The Mad King*), as did John Buchan (*The House of the Winds*) and even Winston Churchill (*Savrola*). Hope himself had more than thirty novels published, most of which are now forgotten. But for would-be duellists, his swashbuckling masterpiece remains the ultimate textbook. *En garde!*

ANTHONY GARDNER is the author of two novels, *Fox* and *The Rivers of Heaven*, and a collection of poetry, *The Pool and Other Poems*. He has never met his doppelgänger, though he was once mistaken for someone called Tony in an American roadhouse.

Sarah Woolfenden

. . . *from the Trees*

ISABEL LLOYD

In Issue 75, I said some books help you grow. Others help you let go.

*

Our son was 17 when he disappeared. I'll call him R. We bought our place that was big enough to plant trees when he was 14. We thought this was a good thing; he loved trees, so did we. While we were busy planting an orchard, a forest garden, he explored the ancient woodland that surrounded us, taking an axe, a tinder box and a bivvy bag. We wouldn't see him again until dark, sometimes not even then.

Three years later, R broke. His exam results were so bad, his school kicked him out. He stopped smiling, stopped seeing friends. He asked to go to a crammer but after six weeks began playing truant, spending his days on a park bench while the college sent me angry text messages. He hated the work; I helicoptered wildly, checking on him constantly, 'helping' him with things he should have been doing himself. The black waters of depression closed over my son; he disappeared beneath them.

We tried to get him excited about our planting plans. But he fought with us continually, telling us off for 'interfering' with nature:

E. Annie Proulx, *Barkskins* (2016): Fourth Estate · Pb · 736pp · £9.99 · ISBN 9780007232017; Richard Powers, *The Overstory* (2018): Vintage · Pb · 640pp · £9.99 · ISBN 9781784708245; Suzanne Simard, *Finding the Mother Tree* (2021): Penguin · Pb · 368pp · £10.99 · ISBN 9780141990286; Oliver Rackham, *Trees and Woodland in the British Landscape* (1976): Weidenfeld & Nicolson · Pb · 272pp · £16.99 · ISBN 9781474614047; Isabella Tree, *Wilding* (2018): Picador · Pb · 384pp · £9.99 · ISBN 9781509805105; Roger Deakin, *Wildwood* (2007): Penguin · Pb · 416pp · £9.99 · ISBN 9780141010014 any time we got the mower out, or the chainsaw, we could expect a meltdown. 'Why can't you just leave things alone?' he yelled.

One cold, rain-pelting March night he ran off and didn't come back until the following morning. He told us he was too anxious to talk to people he knew, even people who loved him. He said he was going to go to Canada to live in the woods.

*

They may be separate books, but together *Barkskins* (2016) by E. Annie Proulx and Richard Powers's *The Overstory* (2018) are a tragedy of trees in three acts. *Barkskins* is set mostly in Canada, *The Overstory* belongs entirely to the USA. But they have the same pain at their heart: the destruction of the great primary North American forests, boreal and temperate, that once stretched unbroken from coast to coast. These were the forests that, in 2018, my son went to live in, and out of which I worried he would never emerge.

I began reading *Barkskins* the day R flew to Canada. It tells, blow by wrenching axe blow, how seventeenth-century Europeans felled the wilderness, displaced the First Nations and founded the New World on timber. As Proulx's two French arrivals walk green and afraid into the woods, I walked with them, feeling the forest R had fled to growing around me.

Then I read *The Overstory*, a narrative of nine environmental protestors fighting the final despoilment of the North American forests from the 1960s on. All were tree-lovers, like R: some hippies, some scientists. One, a character called Patricia Westerford, had an extraordinary theory that trees communicate, that they are connected.

*

After weeks of silence, R finally got in touch. He'd been camping in unpeopled forest two hours north of Vancouver, taking no tent, just a hammock, a knife and a plastic bag filled with rice and peanut butter. The moss and lichen on the forest floor were amazing, he said, so deep your feet sank into them. The insect life was inescapable, the air thick with birdsong. He'd made his camp by a river, where he washed his clothes and dried them on a stone. He'd seen a bear on the opposite bank. The bear had tried to attack him. He hadn't wanted to use bear spray because it would hurt the bear, but when it charged at him, he had to. He didn't like hurting living things.

A few weeks later he texted again, to say he was staying with an elderly couple somewhere called Lillooet; they were homesteaders, living off-grid and growing their own food. The homesteaders were kind, R said, they were hippies; they told him how they had spent their lives campaigning against 'clear-cutting', where foresters felled every tree in an area and sprayed it with weedkiller to clear the scrub. The loggers would then replant what had been a millennia-old habitat of incomprehensible complexity with just one or two profitable species of trees. And these little trees kept dying.

*

Patricia Westerford would say trees die when they can't communicate. So would Suzanne Simard, a 60-year-old Canadian forest ecologist, who is the direct inspiration for Powers's campaigning scientist. Her ground-breaking paper on how trees share resources via soil-borne fungal threads made the cover of *Nature* in August 1997, the moment the world first heard the phrase wood-wide web.

For decades others wrote about her work. But in 2021 Simard's *Finding the Mother Tree: Discovering the Wisdom of the Forest* was published. The title sounds fluffy, but the book is quite the opposite. In it she describes a tough, backwoods childhood, growing up as part of a century-old dynasty of loggers in Lillooet (yes, R's refuge). In her twenties she begins working for the forestry industry, where her job is to work out why, despite careful nurturing, so many young trees turn up their toes. Intrigued by the mycorrhizal threads she sees wrapped around the roots of the few trees that are healthy, she switches direction and moves into academia; what follows are vivid, honest and exhilarating walk-throughs of the forest-based experiments that helped her develop her theories.

After her first, Darwin-busting discovery that different species of trees feed each other, Simard's game-changing insights keep coming. Old, giant specimens – so-called 'mother trees' – use the mycorrhizal network to pipe resources from their failing bodies to the saplings that grow at their feet. Trees of one species under attack from pests or diseases send signals through the network to other species, triggering defensive behaviour such as increasing the amount of bitter tannins in their leaves. The signalling mimics the electrical firing across nerve synapses. In Simard's telling, forests are not a collection of discrete and lonely individuals but a society, interacting, communicating and supporting one another. The soil at their feet is their source, their medium, their neural network. A forest is the unique, uncontrollable and inevitable expression of its soil.

*

In late February 2020, R came home. He'd been surviving, just, in a violent, alcohol-blighted First Nation town deep in the Arctic Circle. His attempt to get Canadian citizenship had failed, he was exhausted and despairing. Three weeks later, England went into lockdown and we spent much of the next year walking, and talking, in the woods.

*

To read a wood, first read Oliver Rackham. A Fellow of Corpus Christi, Cambridge, who died, aged 75, in 2015, he was both a botanist and a historian, incomparably knowledgeable about woodlands and how humans have used them from prehistory on. He was also prodigious – even the most industrious ecology student will struggle to read everything Rackham wrote – but the seeds of all his work are contained in *Trees and Woodland in the British Landscape: The Complete History of Britain's Trees, Woods and Hedgerows*, first published in 1976.

The book is episodic, a collection of short discourses that include pollen analysis of the Neolithic wildwood and comparisons of intensely managed medieval woods with their surviving modern remnants. Rackham is readable, but not forgiving: deeply donnish, often impatient, he shows respect only for documented fact, and he assumes his readers are as botanically minded as he is. But his insights are unforgettable. Through him I learnt of a floating Bronze Age village in the Fens, four acres across, supported on woven wood rafts; of how Dutch Elm Disease in the 1970s echoed a great Elm Decline that wiped out half the trees in Europe in 4,000 BC; of how a wood is designated 'ancient' not because the trees in it are old, but because it has always been a wood.

This stuck with me. In the woods where R and I walked, it is the soil that is ancient. Over hundreds, thousands of years, locals have kept cutting the trees, for timber or for firewood. But then, bedded in their soil, the trees regrow. From stumps, from suckers or from seed. No one has planted anything, but the woods know how to survive.

In 1990, Rackham ended the second edition of *Trees and Woodland* with a warning about the predilection for planting new woods. 'Planting is not conservation', he huffs, but 'an admission that conservation has failed . . . Conservation is about letting trees be trees, not gateposts with leaves.'

*

R and I talked about Rackham's idea of leaving the land alone. Then I read Isabella Tree's *Wilding: The Return of Nature to a British Farm* (2018), and R, his dad and I went to see for ourselves the eruption of life that has filled Knepp estate since Tree and her husband left nature to its own devices.

R rebuilt my old polytunnel and started growing plants from seed. A year later, we kicked the sheep off what we'd always called R Field, the sloping one that backs on to the big woods, and stopped mowing it for hay. We let it be. Young sprigs of hornbeam and poplar have begun to appear in the damp ground by the ditch, growing from seed stored in the soil. In the next field along, I'd planted 250 oaks, small-leaved lime, holly, alder and hornbeam, leaving a clearing in the middle as a spot for growing mushrooms. Fungi from fungi. Even as I did it, I knew it was our last project. From now on, the trees that grow at our home will arrive through their own volition.

*

Rackham taught and inspired many tree-people, not least Roger Deakin, friend of the earth, wild swimmer and passionate nature writer. *Wildwood: A Journey through Trees* (2007) was his final collection of essays, published a year after his death. Witty, lyrical, eccentric, it is as much poetry as it is ecology.

Deakin, a man who would sleep in a ditch in a wood so that he could be woken at dawn by rooks, learnt botany and lepidoptery at school, and he takes care to be correct in the naming of trees and their habitats. But he is also submerged in their beauty, their complexity and otherness. For him, experiencing nature only begins with names. Recognizing a species well enough to name it is like learning the first words in a language. As you develop awareness of the complexity of forest ecosystems, of the vastness of their interdependence – how insect, animal and plant life are woven together, like fungi and roots – you realize you're dealing with something beyond words. Like poetry, trees become an expression of something you can only approach circuitously; they cannot be named, only described.

*

R's name is not R; it is something else. Slowly, he has come back to us. Today, here, now, he grows things for a living.

It's been more than thirty years since I looked at a wood in Germany and wondered what the trees were called. I have broken spades and my back planting something approaching 2,000 trees, when I now know they could have found their way here on their own. Yes, my Collins Gem taught me to name trees, but it took many other books, and many more years, for me to begin to comprehend them. And to know that perhaps the worst thing you can do with a tree – or a person – is to try to control it. Just let it grow.

ISABEL LLOYD is co-author of *Gardening for the Zombie Apocalypse: How to Grow Your Own Food When Civilization Collapses – Or Even if It Doesn't* (2019).

A Recording Angel

ANTHONY QUINN

From the long shelf of books about London that I keep (and keep adding to) the one I most cherish is *The London Nobody Knows*. Published sixty years ago, it is part whimsical vade mecum, part urban elegy, a book that celebrates the lesser-known nooks and corners of a capital that was in drastic transition. Knocked about by German bombing twenty years earlier, London had then come under sustained assault from planners and developers largely inimical to the architectural quirks and anomalies of the Victorian age. The author, Geoffrey Fletcher (1923–2004), was working against the clock: the 'tawdry, extravagant and eccentric' place he loved was fast disappearing, and a recording angel like himself needed his wits about him if he was to preserve its memory. The year of the book's appearance, 1962, had already seen the destruction of two major landmarks, the Euston Arch and the Coal Exchange. More were bound to follow.

Fletcher had a learned eye for architecture, and a fine instinct for comedy. 'I have always been a keen connoisseur of Victorian lavatories,' he declares, and focuses on one such convenience in Star Yard, Holborn, dating from 1897 and still in operation. He discovers from the attendant that a previous incumbent used the cast-iron water tanks to keep his pet fish; each time the stalls were flushed the fish found themselves suddenly coming down in the world – a 'delightfully rococo' idea. He wonders what the men using the place thought of the fish, and 'more importantly, what the fish thought of the men'.

Geoffrey Fletcher, *The London Nobody Knows* (1962)
The History Press · Pb · 144pp · £9.99 · ISBN 9780750995979

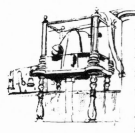

He is startled to learn that these conveniences are known in the trade as 'Queen Victorias', instancing further examples in the Strand and Trafalgar Square, though Holborn remains a favourite, 'for the gas jets are still intact over the water closets, and there are electric bulbs of Edwardian date which bend over like white tulips'.

From low he would go high, to Butterfield's church of All Saints in Margaret Street, with its 'soaring, green-slated spire', or to William Burges's magnificent Tower House in Melbury Road, Kensington, with its stained-glass windows and Virginia creeper 'mantling the conical tower in red, gold and amber'. He is too late to catch the strange and imposing Columbia Market, Victorian Gothic *in excelsis* and yet redolent of 'a medieval cloth hall, with a gatehouse and cloisters'. It came down in the 1950s, a loss he calls 'incalculable'. And yet, against the odds, some of the buildings he hymns survive to this day. Only last week I went down to Eastcheap to behold the 1870s office buildings that stand proud among the steel and glass moderns of the City. They actually look more ecclesiastical than anything to do with commerce. 'Fantastic Victorian Gothic at its most assured', he calls it, a beautiful riot of coloured brick, stone and ironwork – and a sight to make the heart sing.

If Fletcher had been only a writer his achievement would resonate. But, being a former student of the Slade, he also drew, and his illustrations (that Holborn loo included) enliven the pages of *The London Nobody Knows*. His drawings first appeared in the *Manchester Guardian* in 1950 before he became a long-term contributor to the *Daily Telegraph*. Better perhaps to think of him as a latter-day Max Beerbohm, although his drawing style is closer to that of Ronald Searle, minus the ludic spikiness. From both his prose and his pictures we may form

Interior of
Holborn lavatory

an impression of the man, on the stroll through his beloved city, eye always on the alert. He favours what were then the less fashionable districts – Hoxton, Stepney, Shoreditch – investigating the doss-houses and dining-rooms, the obscure pubs and old curiosity shops. If you ever wondered what it might be like to eat in an eel pie saloon, where the tiled walls are lined with mirrors and the mashed potato comes stained with liquor 'like verdigris', this is your guide.

In his foreword to a 2011 reprint of the book the historian Dan Cruickshank calls Fletcher 'an outsider . . . unclubbable', and yet it might be just this solitariness which attracts him to the market porters, the street vendors, the itinerant musicians and pavement artists whose presence lend the city its particular character. Most of them have since gone the way of the muffin men and crossing sweeps of the Victorian age, but Fletcher catches them for posterity here and in later volumes such as *London's Pavement Pounders* (1967).

The most poignant ghosts, however, are those of the music halls and their performers – Marie Lloyd, Dan Leno, George Leybourne (aka Champagne Charlie), and the rest. Fletcher was especially devoted to the New Bedford on Camden High Street, immortalized in etchings and paintings by Sickert. In the 1967 film adapted from *The London Nobody Knows* the narrator – a mournful James Mason – stands inside the blackened ruins of the theatre, awaiting demolition, and muses on its happier days. It will soon become part of the London Nobody Remembers, and aftercomers will have to guess at how it was. Not quite yet, though – a 90-year-old friend of mine still recalls visits to the Bedford in her student youth, when Donald Wolfit and his company did Shakespeare there at 'popular prices'.

Camden is one of two districts that merit their own chapter. The other is Islington, another favourite haunt of Sickert, where the rackety, tumbledown life of old is fleetingly visible in dining-rooms and shops: 'What they sold originally is impossible to say, but they belong to the time when apprentices slept under the shop counter and had to take down the shutters for their first job of the day.' As ever one catches at the corner of Fletcher's eye little dabs of Dickens and Henry Mayhew in the throwback to street life, in the drama of buying and selling. The 1960s momentarily carry the whiff of the 1860s. Chapel Market is a gift to his artist's sense of colour: 'the blue-pink of plucked chicken, partridges, and pheasants touched with dull reds and Prussian blue and occasionally a black and white hare . . .'.

Across Upper Street, the bustle of Camden Passage is apparently trading up to the genteel, for 'the antique dealers have moved in' and the junk shops sent packing. The toy shop and the 'dolls' hospital' have gone the same way. Islington also boasted a famous music hall, the Collins's, by 1962 a burnt-out shell; only the walls of the pub next door tell of its former life in pasted playbills, 'like messages from a lost world – near in time but as defunct as the baked clay tablets from Babylon'. Now the pub has vanished too.

And there is the melancholy double-vision of this book. Fletcher's gaze surveyed a pre-1914 London that was 'essentially a domestic city' in which the unconsidered trifles of architectural invention were simply part of the fabric. Now we look back on Fletcher's own time as one of innocence tinged with ominous warnings. In 1962 Britain was just emerging from the austerity years, the Beatles were about to release their first single and a new spirit of liberation flourished in the wake of the *Lady Chatterley* trial. But the desire to sweep away the old tragically brought doom upon the environment: buildings and streetscapes still serviceable, and often irreplaceable, were torn down in the name of modernization.

The Victorian Society, led by Nikolaus Pevsner, was battling to save St Pancras Station from the wrecking ball, having failed to stop it up the road at Euston. Dan Cruickshank wonders why Fletcher was so 'fatalistic' about change, arguing that he could have used his book 'not just to stimulate people to *look* before all was lost but also to *fight* to save what was left'. This was, he notes, in marked contrast to John Betjeman, who wrote *and* campaigned on behalf of conservation.

While one can understand Cruickshank's disappointment, it might be argued in Fletcher's defence that he was already in the fight: the very publication of *The London Nobody Knows* constituted an act of protest, if not of actual engagement. In a later volume, *London Souvenirs* (1973), he wrote, 'We may not have much hope of saving London and its adjoining areas, but at least we ought not to let them get away with it, without reasoned protest, without thought.' His words and drawings were the arms of his crusade, an alternative to placards, marches and open letters to *The Times*. No one could accuse him of slacking, either. As well as painting and teaching he wrote around thirty books in his lifetime, some of them still to be found online. Geoffrey Fletcher's drawings are themselves now 'messages from a lost world', but in their modest, intricate way they have rescued London's bygone beauty from the darkness of forgetting.

ANTHONY QUINN's latest novel is *London, Burning*. He is now at work on a saga about three generations of artists, from the 1780s to 1983, entitled *Molly & the Captain*.

The last of the Columbia Market, Bethnal Green

The Thread that Binds Them

URSULA BUCHAN

Some years ago, when writing a gardening article for an achingly right-on newspaper, I used the expression 'other men's flowers'. I cannot now remember in what context but I have not forgotten the sub-editor changing the phrase to 'other people's flowers'. I had foolishly imagined that, even if my readers did not know Montaigne – 'I have gathered a posie of other men's flowers and nothing but the thread that binds them is my own' – they would at least recognize the play on the title of one of the great poetry anthologies of the twentieth century. Some hope.

Other Men's Flowers (1944) is a deeply personal anthology compiled by Archibald Percival Wavell, otherwise known as Field Marshal Earl Wavell, GCB, GCSI, GCIE, CMG, MC. We have on our shelves a copy of the attractively produced 'memorial edition', put together two years after his death in 1950, with an introduction by his son, also Archibald. Our volume has an inscription on the flyleaf, which was written by my brother to my husband, and was given to him as a present for acting as an usher at his wedding in 1977. I cannot imagine many young men giving this anthology as a present these days, although I am mighty glad my brother did.

Field Marshal Wavell was a remarkable man. Those letters after his name tell the tale succinctly: Order of the Bath; Grand Commander of the Star of India; Knight Grand Commander of the Order of the Indian Empire; Companion of the Order of St Michael and St

A. P. Wavell (ed.), *Other Men's Flowers: An Anthology of Poetry* (1944)
Pimlico · Pb · 448pp · £16.99 · ISBN 9780712653428

George; Military Cross. Born in 1883, the son of a soldier, he gained a scholarship to Winchester College – then, as now, one of the brainiest public schools in the country – and went on to the Royal Military College, Sandhurst. He joined the Black Watch and served with distinction in both the Second Boer War and the Great War, gaining the Military Cross but losing an eye during the Second Battle of Ypres in 1915. Much of his army career, however, was spent as a staff officer, and his exceptional capabilities of brain and personality made him a very successful one. (He understood well the mutual incomprehension that has always existed between staff and regimental officers; he included in his anthology Hotspur's deeply unflattering account of a 'popinjay', a staff officer in Shakespeare's *Henry IV, Part I*.)

Wavell was given a variety of military jobs between the wars and then, in the summer of 1939, he was made up to a full general when he became GOC Middle East Command, later becoming Commander-in-Chief India, with the task of facing the Japanese threat after Pearl Harbor. He was appointed Viceroy of India towards the end of 1943, at a time of great difficulties, but was sacked by Winston Churchill's successor, Clement Attlee, in 1947, just before Independence, being replaced by a lesser man, Earl Mountbatten. He died three years later and is buried in the cloister garth at Winchester College.

Despite the extreme pressures under which he laboured during the Second World War, Wavell managed to put together *Other Men's Flowers*, which was published by Jonathan Cape. (It is much to the credit of the publishers that they brought the book out in wartime, but it was a shrewd move, for *Other Men's Flowers* was an immediate success and was to be found in many a kitbag taken across to France on D-Day.) Wavell's son wrote in the introduction to the 1952 memorial edition:

> In the brief respite of six months between staving off the German assault on the Middle East in the Spring of 1941, and turning to meet the challenge of Japan at the end of the year, my father found time to list his favourite poems and explain his choice in the prefaces to each section. The family all made their suggestions, and we reminded him of poems we knew he loved but had forgotten to include: the poems that we heard read to us as children . . . So it all began as an idea for a family conversation but we gradually prevailed upon him to let the world join in, and the literary members of his Staff nurtured the conspiracy with the publishers.

An influential member of that Staff was Lieutenant-Colonel Peter Fleming, the travel writer and adventurer. Brother of Ian Fleming and husband of the actress Celia Johnson, he was author of *Travels in Tartary*, also published by Cape. There is something rather wonderful about the C-in-C India talking poetry with his subordinates in the middle of a war that at the time the Allies were at grave risk of losing. Yet even without the anthology, Lord Wavell confounds conventional expectations about the bluff military man only interested in war. He explained in the introduction to the first edition that he had always read poetry

> and since I had once a very retentive memory for verse much has remained in my head . . . I ask no one to applaud my choice. I do not always applaud it myself, but a part of me from which I cannot dissociate myself, my memory, has made this selection and I am too old to alter it. On the whole I think it is a reasonable choice from the almost inexhaustible treasure of English poetry, for a workaday man who prefers plain gold, silver or metal work to elaborate jewellery.

Hardly 'workaday'. The selections are arranged by theme: 'Music, Mystery and Magic', 'Love and All That', 'The Call of the Wild', 'The Lighter Side' and so on. The collection is heavy with Rudyard Kipling, Lord Macaulay, G. K. Chesterton and Sir Walter Scott, as you would expect, but there is much Robert Browning as well. George Herbert and James Shirley find a place but he does not seem to have loved either Wordsworth or Tennyson enough to include them. Where you do find a predictable poet, the poem chosen is often not the most obvious one: no 'Goblin Market' from Christina Rossetti, no 'The Lake Isle of Innisfree' from W. B. Yeats. With the exception of poems by John Masefield, Walter de la Mare and A. E. Housman, there is little or nothing written after the Great War.

As well as introductions to each chapter, there are short notes to some of the entries. These add much to the appeal of the collection, for they often explain why he liked a particular poem or they clear up some mystery for his readers. Occasionally, they are very poignant. After Rupert Brooke's 'The Dead' (you know the one, '. . . Dawn was theirs,/ And sunset, and the colours of the earth') Wavell noted: 'I can well remember Lord Allenby repeating this poem to me shortly after he had heard the news that his only son, a boy of great promise, had been killed in action.' Wavell comes across as a humane and sensitive man. (He also had an excellent sense of humour. I particularly enjoyed the fragment of parody of 'If' that he quotes: 'If you can keep your girl while all about you are losing theirs, and blaming it on you . . .')

Some choices may strike a contemporary readership as a little strange. For example, there are two Julian Grenfell poems but nothing by Wilfred Owen. But Wavell never claimed that this was a comprehensive *tour d'horizon*. He wasn't trying to flatter some unknown audience or pursue any particular fashion or vogue. He was simply pleasing himself, recalling the poetry that he had first read and learned by heart in youth; in doing so, he has pleased every generation since 1944, for this book has never gone out of print.

From the touching and thoughtful introduction in our memorial edition, it is also clear that his son had obviously inherited his father's highly tuned sensibilities. He wrote that poetry mitigated his father's disappointment in 1947. Archibald *fils* confessed to liking rather more modern verse than his father did, including poets that don't find any place here, such as T. S. Eliot and W. H. Auden. A commissioned officer himself, he died the following year (1953) on active service in Kenya during the Mau-Mau uprising. And thus did the earldom of Wavell become extinct.

Field Marshal Wavell wrote in his introduction, in New Delhi in April 1943: 'My experience is that one can never properly appreciate a poem until one has got it by heart: memory stumbles over a word or a line and so wonders why the poet wrote it so, and then savours it slowly that its meaning and relish may stay.' He admitted to declaiming poetry on his daily horse-ride. These days, the lack of encouragement to schoolchildren to learn any poetry by heart means that a vast world of delight, fascination, wisdom and enjoyment is denied them – probably for their lifetimes. How could recent generations have let their young down so badly? This is one area of life that our forebears understood so much better than us. I know how difficult it is to learn a new poem after the age of 60, yet how much I should like to be able to declaim more of the verse I love when walking the dog each day. If you read *Other Men's Flowers*, I hope that you will conclude, as I did, that the wonderful heritage of poetry in English contributed to the making of an eminently civilized man, and both consoled and encouraged him in some pretty dark days.

URSULA BUCHAN is a writer and a lover of poetry, but she could not possibly be a poet. You can also hear her in Episode 9 of our podcast, 'Well-Cultivated Words', on the history of garden writing.

Reaping the Whirlwind

RICHARD PLATT

A warm summer day in 1987. A thump on my doorstep announces the arrival of a stout parcel with the familiar return address, BOMC, Book-of-the-Month Club. These were the pre-Internet days, when BOMC worked exclusively by mail. You had to open the brochure that arrived every three or four weeks and return the postcard that proclaimed you *didn't* want the next month's selection, or else it would be sent automatically. Having neglected to return the postcard, I found myself holding *Freedom* by William Safire, a 1,000-page novel about Abraham Lincoln and the first two years of America's four-year Civil War, this account ending with Lincoln's signing of the Emancipation Proclamation. It was a book I did not want and had no interest in. Still, it was here. I was here. There was no harm in having a look before I sent it back. I sat down and began to read. Three hours later I was still reading. *Freedom* would alter the trajectory of my reading for the next twenty years.

Thomas Jefferson famously said that slavery was like holding a wolf by the ears: you didn't like it much, but you didn't dare let it go. *Freedom* is the story of how America let go of the wolf and came perilously close to committing suicide in the process. I have long been a fan of historical fiction, but I always find myself wondering, as I do when watching a movie or mini-series 'inspired by actual events', where the boundary comes in the shadowland that divides fiction and history. I read or watch and ask, 'How do they know that?

William Safire, *Freedom: A Novel of Abraham Lincoln and the Civil War* (1987), is out of print but we can obtain second-hand copies.

How much is reasonable conjecture, how much demonstrable fact, how much pure fabrication? What were their sources?' Safire gives us a hint in his Note to the Reader.

> In general, the credibility quotient is this: if the scene deals with war or politics, it is fact; if it has to do with romance, it is fiction; if it is outrageously and obviously fictional, it is fact.

Safire, to my knowledge, is unique among historical novelists in that he not only provides a superb, annotated bibliography but also exhaustive endnotes, which he calls the 'Underbook'. In it, he guides the reader chapter by chapter through the original source material. Many of the participants kept diaries, wrote memoirs or had voluminous correspondence, so much of the dialogue in *Freedom* is lifted directly from primary sources. Where philosophical, political or historical controversy arises (and there are controversies aplenty) Safire gives us all sides of the issue and the evidence available to us, then tells us what he thinks and why.

The curtain rises on Washington DC, April 1861. Having snuck into the nation's Capitol in disguise because of threats to his life, Abraham Lincoln, a president with only two years of national political experience as a one-term congressman from Illinois, elected in a four-way race with fewer than four votes in ten, and having not carried a single slave-holding state, yet pledged by his party platform to protect the institution of slavery where it exists, finds himself the chief executive of only half a country, for the southern states are already equipping armies to defy the national authority and perhaps even sack Washington. Despite his often-repeated appeal for calm, the prospect of peace is slipping through his grasp like sand. As he has said to the southern states in his first inaugural address, yet again resorting to reason where reason will not be heard, his high, clear, twangy drawl carrying over the crowd in the shadow of the still unfinished US Capitol dome:

I have no purpose, directly or indirectly, to interfere with the institution of slavery in the States where it exists. I believe I have no lawful right to do so, and I have no inclination to do so . . . In your hands, my dissatisfied fellow-countrymen, and not in mine, is the momentous issue of civil war. The Government will not assail you. You can have no conflict without being yourselves the aggressors. You have no oath registered in heaven to destroy the Government, while I shall have the most solemn one to 'preserve, protect, and defend it'.

And the war came.

It was this last idea, the preservation of the union and the idea that popular government was not an absurdity, to which Lincoln held fast with an almost mystical devotion, and for which he would accept any sacrifice as sectional conflict turned to war, and war to revolution. By war's end that would mean more than 600,000 casualties.

A brief glance at the map on the endpapers will reveal the perilous situation the newly inaugurated president faced. Washington DC was surrounded by Virginia and Maryland, both slave-holding states with legislatures hostile to the incoming president. The Virginia legislature had already voted to secede from the union. The Maryland legislature was planning to convene and follow suit. What was the beleaguered president of an imperilled nation to do? Arrest the entire Maryland legislature *for a crime they were going to commit?* This is the recurring, timeless theme of *Freedom*: how much freedom should citizens of a free nation be willing to relinquish in the name of freedom's preservation?

Alongside the timeless questions there are also wonderful vignettes, all documented fact, reminding us that we are in another world: the President of the United States walking down the street, alone, slopping through the mud of Pennsylvania Avenue in search of a newspaper to give him news of the war. Lincoln, careworn but vigorous, in his early fifties but still immensely strong, driven to such a state of exasperation by a visitor's demands that he actually picks the man up by the belt and collar and throws him from his office, to the vast amusement of his secretaries. And my favourite, another visitor to the presidential residence, only then becoming known as the White House (it has recently been given a belated coat of fresh white paint), finds Lincoln in his office blacking his own boots. When the visitor expresses surprise, the president asks, 'Whose boots should I be blacking?'

If America has a secular saint, that saint is most assuredly Abraham Lincoln. What Safire has done so brilliantly, like a sculptor adding clay in layers until a final likeness emerges, is to reduce Lincoln to human scale and in doing so raise him to greater heights: a man unsure of himself, groping his way forward, struggling with a crippling depression from which he has suffered most of his life, hesitant but obstinate as a mule, ambitious and duplicitous yet altruistic. He is simple in his vulgar and coarse tastes but a canny reader of men and motives who will grow in the office of the presidency as no man has grown before or since. It is the burden of Lincoln's all-too-flawed humanity, his sharp corners, that brings into high relief his quiet heroism. Yet Safire never gushes. As he opines through the voice of Francis Preston Blair, a close adviser of the president's, 'Oh, he's a cunning bastard is Honest Abe.' Indeed.

Safire can speak with some authority on how the wheels of power turn at the highest levels of government – he was once a speechwriter in the White House under Nixon – but he never allows his personality to intrude on the narrative. Other portraits of Lincoln, notably Gore Vidal's bestselling *Lincoln*, published two years before Safire's book, tend to project the character of the author on to the subject. Safire manages to stay out of the way. Though he says in a final endnote that reverence is a barrier to appreciation, ultimately his portrait rings true, laced as it is with both authenticity and admiration, which is only fitting. Admiration is the proper response to greatness.

Since my first reading of *Freedom* I have read many of the highly acclaimed biographies of America's sixteenth president. Now, returning to it thirty-five years later, I see very little in Safire's portrait to quibble with. Mortimer Adler, the guiding spirit behind Columbia University's Great Books programme, said Lincoln had not read a great many books, but he had read a few books really, really well. Anyone privileged to stand within the walls of the Lincoln Memorial, the pillared Grecian temple in Washington that enshrines Lincoln's memory, may attest to this as they read aloud the exquisite prose of the Second Inaugural Address and the Gettysburg Address, both chiselled into the marble walls. I have stood there many times, and on each visit I have been moved to tears. It is a powerfully serene space, as awe-inspiring as a cathedral; a monument to an imperishable memory.

As I put *Freedom* down again, I am left with much the same feeling I have experienced at the Lincoln Memorial: I have been with the man who proved that democracy was not an absurdity, and I have basked in the presence of greatness.

RICHARD PLATT believes the emancipation proclamation is a genre of its own. He's written several things on it himself: see www.RichardPlattAuthor.com.

The Sweetest Note of All Others

WILLIAM PALMER

Most of the houses of East Sheen in south-west London were built on farmland as part of the great explosion of suburbia between the 1890s and 1930s. The houses are solid and the rear gardens long. There are ancient copses in nearby Richmond Park and the surrounding patches of common land but most of the garden trees were planted by the first residents and have grown over the years to maturity, just as the hedges of hawthorn and privet have grown taller and thicker. Patient gardening turns the soil and throws up worms and hundreds of other varieties of insect. A consequence of all this activity is that, with the destruction of wild woodland and the poisoning of farmland by chemical fertilizers, perhaps the safest place for wild birds is now a leafy suburb – apart, that is, from the large number of cats, sitting with deadly patience under hedges and in long grass, but I'll come back to them.

Certainly our garden in East Sheen is visited by blackbirds, goldfinches, jays, crows, magpies, wood pigeons, London pigeons, hedge sparrows, blue tits, coal tits and the bright green parakeets that fan out from Richmond Park. (The first parakeets were allegedly brought from Africa to Shepperton Studios to add colour to studio-shot scenes of the film *The African Queen*: some escaped and have bred in

David Lack, *The Life of the Robin* (1943)
Pallas Athene · Pb · 304pp · £12.99 · ISBN 9781843681304
Unfortunately, David Lack's anthology of writings about the robin, *Robin Redbreast* (1950), is hard to find. However, an updated and enlarged version, *Redbreast* (2008), edited by Andrew Lack, though out of print is more commonly available.

the park ever since.) Most birds will feed in the trees or on the ground in our garden, but when a human emerges from the house they immediately fly off to what they judge is a safer distance. The only bird that holds its ground or merely flits away to a nearby hedge to observe us is the robin.

Over the past twenty years we have had several generations of robins nesting in our garden. We grew fond of one in particular. I shall call him 'he' because he did seem to perform the male duty of getting food and taking it back to the nest. The peculiarity of this bird was that he had only one leg. That is to say that he only ever used one leg, the left, to alight on the ground or on the fence, or to hop about. He did have a right leg, but it seemed permanently bent into his side. To try and shed some light on this I hunted through my shelves for an old Pelican book called *The Life of the Robin*, by David Lack. Though it contains only one reference to robins who sometimes perch on one leg (and makes no mention of any who were never seen to use the other), I became engrossed. The book had been too long in that large category of books consulted in some way but never actually read all the way through. I'm very glad I did with this one.

The Life of the Robin was first published in 1943, and a revised edition followed in 1953. It is one of the few Pelicans of that time whose chaste blue and white cover has a splash of another colour – the red breast of the robin. It was intended as a serious study, based on Lack's four years of observing robins at Dartington in South Devon before the Second World War, but it was written primarily for the non-scientific bird-lover, and was concerned with the real life of the robin, 'which may be found more curious than the legends'. Not that Lack ignored the legends and the representation of robins in literature; in 1950 he followed his study with *Robin Redbreast*, a wonderful anthology of the bird's appearances in folklore, poetry and children's literature over the centuries.

The most abiding countryside legend has always been that the wife of the cock robin is the smaller wren, little Jenny Wren – a mistake easily made, as the two species often live in close proximity, but in fact the male and female robin appear indistinguishable. Lack first sexed his birds largely by their behavioural patterns: because robins are unusually trusting, he was able to trap, ring and release over a hundred birds with a combination of coloured rings so that he could easily identify any single bird of either sex.

Over the years he mapped out their patterns and rituals. Like most creatures, a robin's life involves the challenges of survival when young, forming a partnership, establishing a home and territory where food can be gathered and, above all, fighting in defence of its ground. A male robin seeking to enter another's territory will quickly be met at the boundary and the two birds will engage in a contest of loud song and dramatic posturing with much display of their red breasts – rather like two rival tenors at La Scala. Except for very young aggressive robins, it is rare for such displays to result in actual physical combat. Usually the would-be usurper is seen off and slinks away to sing rather forlornly from a distance, while the victor sings loudly in triumph. Lack points out sardonically that 'it is rare indeed in intelligent man that a territorial dispute is settled bloodlessly'. Man's use on the battlefield of musical aggression in the form of drums, pipes and martial songs usually results in mass bloodshed; the robin's mellifluous song results in our pleasure. As Goldsmith said, of all British birds 'it has the sweetest note of all others'.

Why we take particular pleasure in the songs of the robin is still rather mysterious. After all, most noises birds make are rudimentary calls of alarm or aggression, such as the repetitive chants of the seagull. It is easy to anthropomorphize the actions of animals we like, but the songs of robins are often more individually recognizable and more musically complex than would seem necessary for their simple purposes.

Jill Meager

Victorious in battle, the robin sings long and loud; but on first acquiring his own territory his song is also a way of advertising his availability as a mate. It is the hen birds who seek out their mates, rather than the other way about. Sadly, cock birds tend to sing a great deal less after pairing up and hen birds sing hardly at all. It sounds like many a suburban marriage.

After the birds have paired, the breeding season starts in early spring. Cup-shaped nests are constructed by the female from moss and leaves and usually concealed in a crevice or a hollow in the ground, but they can be built in some very odd places: 'a jam-jar, an old boot, a pulpit, a human skull . . . a gardener hung up his coat in the tool shed at 9.15 a.m., and when he took it down to go off to lunch at 1 p.m. there was an almost complete robin's nest in one of the pockets'.

The case of the nest in the skull echoes the old country legend that robins cover the dead with leaves. This seems to have originated in the sixteenth century but may be much older. Early graveyards were often not kept in good order and it may have been the sight of robins flitting down to examine freshly turned earth that started the belief that they were somehow attending to the dead. In *Cymbeline*, Shakespeare has the 'ruddock' bring down flowers to sweeten the grave of Imogen, and 'furred moss besides, when flowers are none,/ To winter-ground thy corpse'. The full glory of the legend is seen in the ballad 'The Children in the Wood' by that great poet Anon., which first appeared in the late seventeenth century. A young girl and boy are wickedly abandoned in a wood:

> Thus wandered these poor innocents,
> Till death did end their grief;
> In one another's arms they died,
> As wanting due relief:
> No burial this pretty pair
> From any man receives,
> Till robin redbreast piously
> Did cover them with leaves.

As Lack points out, in much later Christmas pantomime versions of *The Babes in the Wood*, the children are of course rescued by none other than Robin Hood.

Indeed, it's at Christmas that the robin comes into his own with his appearance on millions of greetings cards. On early Victorian cards a robin is often seen holding a letter in its beak or lifting the knocker on a front door, and on one card the heading above the robin is 'The Little General Postman'. And 'Robin' had by the 1850s become a common nickname for postmen since they wore a bright red coat as part of their uniform. In Trollope's *Framley Parsonage* (1861), Jemima the cook calls out in welcome, 'Come in Robin postman, and warm theeself awhile.'

When reading the legends and poetry – by Skelton, Herrick, Wordsworth, Coleridge, Keats and Clare, among many others – that celebrate the beauty of the bird's song, its plucky bearing and seeming fondness for human company, it is easy to forget that the life of these birds has always been precarious.

When young robins hatch in spring, and their parents then feed them for a few weeks, what are their future life prospects? For most, very poor. Lack calculated that '57 per cent of the eggs in completed clutches gave rise to young which successfully left the nest'. Of these young birds only 23 per cent survived until they could themselves breed. The average age of the robin is only a little over a year. But, still, as in country churchyards where there are always a few tombstones from the eighteenth and nineteenth centuries recording people of great age, in a time of high mortality among infants, so too there are robins who live for twelve years. And they do live a great deal faster than humans. Anyone who has held a robin in the hand will be astonished by the strength of its beating heart: as Lack found, their pulse rate is over 900 beats a minute, so that 'an 11-year-old robin is equivalent to a man 150 years old'.

The robin lives in easy accommodation with us and can become a little spoiled: 'several tamers of robins have noted the bird's fondness for butter. Three which regularly took butter would not take margarine.' The birds cling still closer to human dwellings in hard winters when food is scarce. This unfortunately brings them into contact with their prize enemy – the domestic cat. Of 110 deaths of robins examined in Lack's book, cats were responsible for 44. I suspect that proportion is even higher in the suburbs. Fortunately, though, in the past few centuries the British have been too fond of their robins to wantonly kill, let alone cook and eat them. I don't know if the French still eat small songbirds, but they certainly did so in the last century. In 1916 a French ornithologist observed that 'in the district of Le Var, round Toulon, the robins destroyed in one season totalled 20,000'. As William Blake wrote:

> The Robin and the Wren
> Are God Almighty's Cock and Hen,
> Him that Harries their nest
> Never shall his soul have rest.

And our own robin with one usable leg? We enjoyed seeing him in the garden for almost three years, but he has not been seen at all for almost a year now. I suspect foul play by a black-and-white cat that hangs about our garden; no doubt greatly loved in his own house, but not in ours.

WILLIAM PALMER is the author of seven novels and two collections of poetry. His latest book, *In Love with Hell: Drink in the Lives and Work of Eleven Writers*, was published in 2021. You can also hear him in our podcast, Episode 38, 'Literary Drinking'.

Quick Brains and Slow Tongues

MATHEW LYONS

My parents are both now dead. My father died last, aged 90, in 2016. I had always associated my love of books with my mother's influence. My father's passing, however, made me realize – too late – that most of the books I turn to for comfort are those to which he introduced me. I can track my childhood through the stories he read to me at bedtime, from Pooh and Alice through to Thurber, Leacock and Conan Doyle. Later came Chandler, Hašek and others. As we grew up, he continued to read some of these aloud to us, snorting with uncontrollable laughter at the jokes.

But no one amused either of us more than Damon Runyon, whose Broadway stories became hugely popular in Britain in the 1930s and '40s, largely thanks to Lord Beaverbrook, who bought the rights to *More than Somewhat*, an early collection, and ran the stories one by one across the centrefold of the *Evening Standard*. Later, two of them were combined to create the hit musical *Guys and Dolls*.

Many of these stories have nicely worked, if rather old-fashioned, plots that marry sentimentality and violence to pleasing effect. In 'The Old Doll's House', for instance, a bootlegger named Lance Mc-Gowan, on the run from rival gangsters, hides in the house of Abigail Ardsley, a famously rich, reclusive old woman. They talk. She tells him how in her youth she fell in love with a clerk. He used to sneak into the house to see her, just as McGowan has. Her father discovered

---

Two collections of Damon Runyon's stories are available in paperback from Penguin: *On Broadway* · 576pp · £20 · ISBN 9780141184234; and *Guys and Dolls and Other Stories* · 288pp · £9.99 · ISBN 9780141188331.

them together one night, the night of a great snowstorm. He threw her lover out. The young man froze to death on their doorstep.

When McGowan leaves, he tracks down his would-be assassins and shoots them. At his trial, everyone is stunned when the notoriously private Miss Ardsley is called as a witness. What time did the defendant leave your house that night? his lawyer asks. Twelve o'clock she says. It's the very moment when McGowan's rivals were murdered across town. The charges are dropped. Only at the end do we learn that Abigail long ago had every clock in the house stopped at midnight – the last time she saw her lover alive.

But one of my favourites, 'Blood Pressure', barely has a plot at all. It's really little more than a picaresque tour of Runyon's world of illicit gambling joints, speakeasies and all-night diners, told, as all the stories are, by a narrator who lives wholly in that world but who affects to be 'a guy who is just around'. Its story is this: the narrator – unnamed, but let's call him Runyon too – is standing on Broadway late one night contemplating his blood pressure. It is too high and he needs to avoid stressful situations. Runyon is accosted by a supremely vicious gangster named Rusty Charley who drags him to two gambling dens and a speakeasy, by way of a breakneck journey in a cab. His stress level gets higher every step of the way. Everyone is afraid of Rusty Charley, Runyon most of all; along the way Charley punches out a taxi driver, five policemen and a horse. At Charley's apartment, his wife blames Runyon for leading her husband astray, hitting him on the head with a brick as he flees the scene. Back at the doctor's, Runyon discovers his blood pressure is down. 'It only goes to show what just a little bit of quiet living will do for a guy,' the doctor tells him.

It's a small world, this. Most stories take place in New York, in the five blocks either side of 50th Street, book-ended by 10th Avenue to the west and Park Avenue to the east. They were largely written in the first half of the 1930s and either look back to Prohibition or are set during the Depression. The rich and glamorous may pass through, but this is essentially a poor man's world of gamblers, dreamers, gangsters and hustlers, most of whom live hand to mouth. 'What Feets Samuels does for a living', Runyon writes of a grifter in one story, 'is the best he can, which is the same thing many other guys in this town do for a living.'

For all that his characters have colourful, almost vaudevillian names – Hot Horse Herbie, The Seldom Seen Kid, Dream Street Rose – and speak an argot all of their own, the world Runyon writes about was a real one. As a 1939 Random House travel guide explains, Broadway was 'the district of glorified dancing girls and millionaire playboys and, on a different plane, of dime-a-dance hostesses and pleasure-seeking clerks . . . [of] gangsters and racketeers, panhandlers and derelicts, youthful stage stars and ageing burlesque comedians, world heavyweight champions and once-acclaimed beggars.' That's Runyon's Broadway to a tee.

It is not a world that Runyon himself was born into, however. Alfred Damon Runyan (the spelling changed later) was born in 1880 in another Manhattan altogether – the hick one in Kansas – the eldest of four children. His mother was consumptive. When she died in 1888, his grandmother came and took Runyon's three younger sisters to live with her. He never saw them again. His father was a drinker and a newspaperman. He and his son shared a room – and a bed – in a boarding-house. The father worked late into the night then headed for the saloon. Coming home at 5 in the morning he would rouse the son from bed so he could sleep the day through. Runyon's schooling was negligible: he learned to read from his father's old newspaper columns. He found for himself what education he needed either in the local library or by watching what happened on the streets. It's not hard to make the leap from such a childhood to an adult who believed that everything in life was transactional.

Respect for money dominates Runyon's world, be it old money

made a generation back by railroad tycoons or the new money of the bootleggers and hoodlums. Life is a game played with weighted dice; anyone who beats them is owed respect. On a train, Runyon and a friend bump into one such man, Mr Phillips Randolph. 'Why . . . he is the sixth richest guy in this country, or maybe the seventh,' the friend says. 'It is a great honor for us to be travelling with Mr Phillips Randolph, because of him being such a public benefactor and having so much dough, especially having so much dough.'

The people most at home in this world are gangsters and horse-players, no matter where they are from, but there are quite a few stories about out-of-towners who are washed up into it. Men like Tobias Tweeney, for example, in 'Tobias the Terrible', who comes to the city from rural Pennsylvania to meet some gangsters because his home-town girlfriend compares him unfavourably with her idols, James Cagney and Edward G. Robinson. When Tobias asks Runyon if he knows such types, he is horrified. 'I do not know any such characters,' he says, 'and if I do know about them I am not going to speak about it, because the best a guy can get in this town if he goes around speaking of these matters is a nice kick in the pants.' The first rule of Broadway is, you don't talk about what goes on on Broadway.

It is, in fact, one of the glories of Runyon's style this, the great propriety and exactitude with which he and his characters avoid saying things directly. Famously, there are no contractions but there are euphemisms aplenty. Saying the wrong thing, doing the wrong thing – heavens, *wearing* the wrong thing – might prove fatal. Rusty Charley 'is known to often carry a gun in his pants pocket, and sometimes to shoot people down as dead as door-nails with it if he does not like the way they wear their hats – and Rusty Charley is very critical of hats'. So naturally, people choose their words carefully. Words mean things; the *wrong* words in particular.

'Runyonese', the critic Ian Hamilton said, was 'a lingo invented to convey the simultaneous workings of a slow brain and a speedy tongue'. But I think that might be the wrong way round. Everyone is thinking fast about what *not* to say. In 'Gentlemen, the King!' a Philadelphia gangster named Kitty Quick approaches Runyon.

'Listen,' he says, 'do you know anybody in Europe?'

Well, this is a most unexpected question, and naturally I am not going to reply to unexpected questions by guys from Philly without thinking them over very carefully, so to gain time while I think, I say to Kitty Quick: 'Which Europe do you mean?'

This is dialogue as prevarication, holding what you know close to your chest while you wait to play out your hand. Everyone who belongs on Runyon's Broadway thinks this way, and it's the one thing they have in common with the way Runyon writes. The formality, the euphemisms, the sensitivity to how words might be received go hand in hand. They are a necessity because everyone, Runyon's narrator included, lives wholly in the present tense. It's what makes them, and the way they live, so attractive, despite their foibles – if homicide can be classed as a foible.

It's a transient world, too; the trajectory of the lives in it is downwards – and they all know it. 'All Horseplayers Die Broke', one story is titled. 'I long ago come to the conclusion that all life is six to five against,' a ticket tout named Sam the Gonoph says in 'A Nice Price'. Jo-Jo, a Chicago gangster and associate of Kitty Quick, is pointed out to visitors to the city as a 'very remarkable guy because he lives as long as he does, which is maybe forty years'.

For all that Runyon's world is long gone, its slang filed away in dictionaries, the stories are so vivid and their sometimes ridiculous characters so alive because the prose still sings in the timeless vernacular of the moment, and the very transience of the lives depicted sharpens the vitality of the language to an exquisite point.

That point, in most stories, is more comic than it is poignant, but it is often poignant nonetheless. I feel that more piercingly than I once did, partly, I think, because I can hear my father's voice more clearly, his delight in the ever-living now of that historic present tense, in the lovely open rhythms of the phrases, which often seem to decline through the cases of a thought towards the definitive expression of an idea. 'As Sam gets older,' it is said of Sam the Gonoph, 'he will not think of stealing anything. At least not much, and especially if it is anything nailed down.'

As I get older, these stories, more than any others that my father introduced me to, allow me to experience again a different historic present, where he is still reading aloud to us and his voice is briefly, keenly real once more.

MATHEW LYONS is a writer and historian who mostly just does the best he can.

A Friendly Looking Lot

POSY FALLOWFIELD

When I was 6 I broke my arm and had to go to hospital to have it set in plaster of Paris. All this, both the breaking and the setting, made for an eventful day. When I got home there on the table was a book, a present to cheer me up (this was 1954 when presents for a not-birthday were perhaps rarer than they are now). The book was *The Bell Family* by Noel Streatfeild and I have it still. It's the story of an impoverished vicar's family who triumph over adversity by being, basically, nicer than their odious rich relations; there's also a cleaning lady called Mrs Gage who has a heart of gold and drops her aitches. It seems very anachronistic now, but at 6 I was a sucker for heart-warming stories about gallant, united families. And I loved the illustrations, which were by Shirley Hughes.

Her line drawings perfectly capture the stoicism, pain or embar-rassment of the put-upon Bells, as well as their good-humoured decency; she conveys just as convincingly the pomposity and snootiness of the cousins. She captures Mrs Gage's affection for the family along with her double chin; she draws truculent children, twinkling adults, stern policemen, indulgent grandmothers. These are thoroughly executed line drawings featuring shabby wallpaper and kitchen sinks and a dog under the table – I attempted to paint some of them, I'm sorry to say, because they were calling out for colour. For me, the characters in the book could not possibly have

---

A number of Shirley Hughes's books, including the *Dogger* and *Alfie* series, are available in paperback from Red Fox. *The Shirley Hughes Collection* (2000) is available from Bodley Head (Hb · 352pp · £19.99 · ISBN 9780370326825).

looked any other way. Shirley Hughes's drawings were the truth, and the reason I treasured the book.

And then, twenty years later, starting to collect books for my own children, I recognized on some of the covers – all in colour now of course – the same look on the faces of both adults and children. It was a good-tempered, equable, making-the-best-of-it look, a look of reality, a look you believed in. Grown up now, with my world fundamentally changed, I was delighted that these people were still around. It was like finding old friends.

Gone now were the cleaning ladies, the post-war frocks (and the vicars). Instead, mums and dads were wearing jeans and harassed expressions, living in not very tidy houses, looking as if they were a bit hard up but – like the Bell family – managing to get by and be cheerful. They were a friendly looking lot, affectionate parents, good neighbours, decent people. No one was glamorous and everyone was drawn truthfully: clothes were rumpled, shoes scuffed, bedrooms muddled; a contented toddler might be gurgling in his buggy, but the mother pushing him would be laden with shopping and looking as if she needed a cup of tea. An adorable chubby baby might be sitting in her high-chair – but would be dropping lumps of food all over the floor, having first put some in her hair. These were people and households one could identify with.

Although her skill enabled her to draw anything – in *The Faber Book of Nursery Stories* (1966) she drew beautiful tigers, bears, apes and mice – Shirley Hughes clearly preferred drawing children, in all their moods. Collaborating with Dorothy Edwards on the *My Naughty Little Sister* series gave her ample rein to show the good, the bad and the grumpy. And having begun by illustrating books for other writers, Hughes soon found that she could write excellent books for children herself; being a mother of three clearly gave her plenty of material.

Over the years she tried various formats – graphic books without any text, like the delightful *Up and Up* (1979) about a little girl flying over the rooftops to evade capture; or *Chips and Jessie* (1985), a mixture of text and comic strip, which gives the impression that she couldn't help launching into a drawing at every opportunity. Towards the end of her long, productive life (she died earlier this year), she even wrote a novel for young adults. But it's her books for young children for which she is best known and probably most loved.

The *Alfie* series features a little boy – too small for school, on one fateful day too small to reach the door-knob – and his younger sister, Annie Rose. Each book describes an event in Alfie's life which any child would recognize as huge. The crises are always resolved (and Alfie is always a little wiser as a result) but what is as satisfying as the resolution is the detail in the illustrations. The pictures are as generous

with information as the text: in *Alfie's Feet* (1982), as he stamps about the house with his new wellies on the wrong feet, we see baby Annie Rose thoughtfully unpacking the shopping basket and arranging vegetables across the floor, unnoticed by Mum (who has slipped off her too-tight shoes under the table) because she is chatting to Dad, while he carefully pours boiling water into the coffee pot. We learn something about each member of the family, and we know this is their reality.

In *Alfie Gets in First* (1981), where Alfie finds himself locked inside the house and Mum locked out – a frightening situation for them both – Hughes cleverly shows us events inside and out on the same double spread. The scene starts quietly with Alfie unsure what to do while Mum calls instructions through the door, but as fear sets in Alfie dissolves into tears while Annie Rose on the outside has a proper meltdown. Gradually the outdoor scene becomes more and more crowded with helpers as Annie Rose's wails get louder – and more and more heads are poked out of windows along the street – while indoors we see Alfie concentrating on carrying his little chair, which is going to enable him to reach the latch. He eventually opens the door and everybody breathes a sigh of relief. The final scene shows all those who'd tried to help crowded into the kitchen having a cup of tea together, Alfie receiving praise as the hero of the hour, Mum looking weary but relieved, Annie Rose cosily tucked up on a neighbour's lap sucking a biscuit. In that drawing of seven individuals you see good humour, kindness to children and a sense of community.

Community is a favourite theme for Hughes. The *Trotter Street* series is all about neighbourliness (reflecting now, in the 1980s, Britain's changing communities) and perhaps this is why most of her stories take place in urban settings. Not for Hughes the idealized farm with spotless animals as background, or the fairytale castle in some distant land – she prefers terraced streets, crowded pavements and small gardens. She shows us parents walking their children to school – never driving – and we feel that the neighbours are all at least on nodding terms. We are not in a fantasy setting where people, according to their deserts, might shrink, turn green or explode. Other writers have made a good living exploring those possibilities, but Shirley Hughes never saw the need to go beyond the world that most children recognize: the neighbourhood and the home, where people are decent, predictable and kind. This is reassuring territory for the small child.

She reflects social change – hardly surprising as she was born in 1927 and in the course of her ninety-four years saw plenty of it. Gradually more and more fathers are seen taking a share in parenting;

in *Dogger* (1977) there is even a father waiting at the school gate (with, admittedly, seven mothers). In *Alfie's Feet* we see a dad carrying a newborn on his chest in a sling (something the Reverend Bell would never have done in 1954). We get the impression that the harassed mothers would like to be more than just mothers. But the kindness is a constant and the people are essentially the same; the stories all conclude, satisfyingly, with a secure and contented child.

There is plenty of sly humour too – but in the illustrations, not the text. In *Helpers* (1975) teenage George, who comes to look after three children for a day, means well but is shown to be useless when it comes to anything practical, unaware of anyone's needs but his own. And in *Dogger*, the illustrations of the egg-and-spoon race and the wheelbarrow race are amusing, but the illustration of the grimly competitive fathers' race is hilarious. Hughes is equally good at illustrating grief: when there's a crisis children howl inconsolably, fists clench, tears spurt. Nowhere does she show this better than at the climax of *Dogger* when an unknown little girl carries off Dave's beloved toy dog and Dave's world threatens to collapse around him: we see a little boy quite desperate with grief. At this point his big sister Bella comes to the rescue, generously saving the day so that poor Dave need howl no more.

This is another of Hughes's themes: the bond of the family. Siblings (like the nameless naughty little sister) can often be maddening but they are siblings nonetheless and *in extremis* they look out for each other. Bella doesn't hesitate to make a sacrifice because she understands the importance of Dogger to her brother – and Nancy in *The Trouble with Jack* (1970) says at the end, 'The trouble with Jack . . . is that as he's my brother I've got to put up with him whatever he's like.'

But always it's the illustrations capturing the mood perfectly; the facial expressions, the stances, the postures tell us everything we need to know. Hughes's small children in all their moods and crises are drawn with such truthfulness – she does a great deal with the positioning of feet, the splaying of fingers, the angle of eyebrows. And she is wonderful at babies – babies surveying the world placidly from their buggies or cots, or sitting on the floor with both legs straight out in front, not quite crawling, all their attention focused on whatever it is they're clutching in their small hands. Even Dogger himself, a little worn and battered, one ear up, one down, is like that because he has always been cuddled on the same side. Her work is clearly the result of years of tireless observation – and a real affection for children. Her children are secure, with the security that comes from being loved. The drawing on the cover of *Alfie and Mum* (2016) says it all: three heads, close together, sharing a story.

It's a good world, Shirley Hughes's world: decent, kind people keeping children safe. There's nothing revolutionary about it, but it's precious. Long may her work be celebrated.

POSY FALLOWFIELD likes nothing more than sharing a book with a lapful of grandchild.

An Olympian Scoundrel

JONATHAN LAW

It's a funny thing, humour. What makes you laugh out loud may leave me with a face like an Easter Island statue. In my own experience the funniest books are non-fiction, and most of these are biographies. There really is nothing so strange or funny as real people. If I had to present my case, then Exhibit A would surely be Bernard Wasserstein's *The Secret Lives of Trebitsch Lincoln* (1988), the extraordinary, meticulous, marvellously funny biography of a man who was – well, what exactly?

In his foreword Wasserstein seeks to explain how a serious academic historian became obsessed by a character he describes as 'part-parasite, part-irritant, part-entertainer'. It all began one afternoon in the mid-1980s, when a summer downpour left Wasserstein stranded in the Bodleian Library. Idly, he started to browse the Index to the General Correspondence of the Foreign Office and looked up a half-remembered name: Ignatius Trebitsch Lincoln. Like a spell, the words opened a portal to another world, with minute after memo after telegram logging the diverse, baffling and always preposterous activities of Trebitsch in locations ranging from Budapest to Shanghai. 'I started to read while waiting for the storm to pass,' writes Wasserstein, '. . . and the tempest has not yet abated.' For several years, he would pursue his anti-hero through archives held in multiple countries which recorded an equally dizzying multiplicity of aliases, frauds, conspiracies and scams. More remarkably still, he

---

Bernard Wasserstein, *The Secret Lives of Trebitsch Lincoln* (1988), is out of print but we can obtain second-hand copies.

would shape this material into a lucid, disturbing and very funny narrative.

Even in its bare bones, the story unearthed by Wasserstein is mind-boggling. Ignácz or Ignatius Trebitsch was born into a Hungarian Jewish family in 1879, and as a young man drifted into a life of petty crime. Having converted to Christianity, he fetched up in Canada, where he became the star preacher of the Montreal Mission to the Jews. As would invariably occur, Trebitsch dazzled with his charm and energy before infuriating everyone with his absurd egotism. By 1903 he was in England, where he added 'Lincoln' to his name as a token of his new passion: politics.

An entrée to this wider world was provided by B. S. Rowntree, the Quaker cocoa magnate, who persuaded him to stand as a Liberal in the General Election of 1910. Sensing his disadvantage as a foreigner, Trebitsch turned his eloquence on the filthy German custom of eating dogs and gained a famous victory. However, he soon stood down to focus on business, having set up a number of dubious companies to exploit the oil boom in central Europe. When the oil ran out, Trebitsch faced ruin and took the fatal step of forging a crucial document. Exposure could only be a matter of time.

Wasserstein pinpoints the next phase as crucial to the birth of Trebitsch Lincoln, International Man of Mystery. With the advent of war, Trebitsch saw a way out of his predicament. Boldly, he called at the War Office and offered to infiltrate German Intelligence as a double agent. He then met German officials and suggested the converse. Before much could come of all this, exposure over the forgery loomed and in 1915 he hightailed it across the Atlantic.

Probably no one but Trebitsch would have thought to deflect a charge of fraud by accusing himself of high treason. In a series of pieces for the US press he built up his inconsequential dealings with the spy agencies into a tale worthy of John Buchan; he had been a foreign agent for years, he now insisted, acting always from a principled hatred of England.

The superspy was duly collared but managed to escape through a lavatory window. Typically, rather than lying low he went to the papers and gave a bombastic press conference. When he was recaptured, his pockets full of press clippings about himself, he congratulated the police on catching 'the cleverest man in America'.

Returned to England, Trebitsch served three years in Parkhurst prison on the Isle of Wight and on his release in 1919 was deported. He went straight to Berlin and there plunged into the atmosphere of febrile conspiracy brewing in right-wing circles. With a grisly crew of confederates, he helped to foment the Kapp Putsch of March 1920 – a bungled coup in which militarists briefly seized control of the state. 'We shall come again,' Trebitsch prophesied, as it all collapsed around him. In the last hours of the putsch he had met a new recruit, a certain ex-corporal who would be rather more than a footnote to history. In Wasserstein's words, the putsch 'began as comic opera and ended as melodrama, but . . . may also be seen as a dress rehearsal for tragedy'. As for Trebitsch himself, the *Daily Telegraph* had few doubts that he would be back:

> There is something almost Olympian about this man's scoundrelism . . . I have heard it variously suggested that he was in the movement as a Bolshevik, as a British, and as a French spy. Possibly he was all these . . . The world will watch with interest to see at what point this really remarkable rogue will crop up next.

Within weeks Trebitsch was in Hungary, at the centre of a still more dangerous plot: the creation of a 'White International' to stir up counter-revolutionary action throughout Europe. Its leaders included White Russian generals and fanatical right-wingers from half a dozen states. Where Trebitsch's earlier associates-cum-dupes had been a mostly herbivorous lot – Quakers, missionaries, Liberals – he was now consorting with terrorists, thugs and murderous anti-Semites.

As a Jew himself, however, Trebitsch began to feel distinctly unsafe and fled to Vienna with a suitcase full of stolen plans. These he attempted to hawk to British and French diplomats, only to be dismissed as a liar and fantasist. He was even arrested by the Austrians for attempted fraud. Meanwhile, he was stalked through the streets of Vienna by White agents seeking his death.

Wisely, Trebitsch decided that it was time for another disappearing act. 'My destination is a profound secret,' he announced, 'I shall disappear as if the earth had swallowed me and shall reappear in an unexpected quarter . . .'

That quarter turned out to be Sichuan province in China, where he surfaced some time in 1922. Not even Wasserstein was able to dig up much about his doings there, but it seems that he served several rival warlords as an arms dealer, loan-broker and all-purpose *consigliere*. China also provided the scene for the last and most astounding phase of Trebitsch's career. By late 1925 he had come to believe that his life had been futile, and so by definition was any kind of worldly activity. 'I made the great renunciation,' he would write, 'I forced the doors of the lunatic asylum open and – walked out.'

For five years Trebitsch immersed himself in the study of Chinese Buddhism, and in 1931 he became a monk, adopting the name Chao Kung. The initiation involved an agonizing ritual in which his shaved head was branded with religious symbols and from this time he dressed in a skull cap and flowing robes. In 1932 he set up his own monastery in Shanghai with thirteen European converts. 'My work is to help suffering humanity,' he proclaimed, 'You are all doomed by your wickedness and folly!'

Not for the first time, we are left wondering what on earth to think. Wasserstein's view is that Trebitsch was quite genuine in his newfound religious convictions, however dodgy his conduct (there would be allegations concerning the younger nuns). Judgement is made more difficult by the way Trebitsch's always fervent self-belief had curdled into something bordering on the psychotic. Not only had he taken to lecturing world leaders on their duties, in the most peremptory terms, but he believed he had a telepathic link to certain 'Supreme Masters' of Tibet, whose spiritual powers made them all but omnipotent. So, for example, at Christmas 1939 he wrote to demand the resignation of every government fighting the war (except the Japanese), as otherwise the Masters would 'unchain forces and powers whose very existence are unknown to you'.

Abbot Chao Kung (aka Trebitsch Lincoln), 1932

Despite claiming to have abjured politics, Trebitsch spent the war years in tortuous, mostly pro-Axis, intrigues and made enemies who could hardly have been more lethal. When the end came, in 1943, it would be in a baffling manner wholly appropriate to the life he had lived. Officially he died from an intestinal complaint, but there were rumours of poison.

The story of Trebitsch Lincoln is by any standards a strange one, but what makes it so very funny? Cheats and scammers are always potentially funny so long as we are not their victims. And then there is Trebitsch's extraordinary personality. He had the *folie de grandeur* of the classic sitcom character – a Tony Hancock or Captain Mainwaring – but on an almost apocalyptic scale. This is the man who admonished King George V that 'millions of Buddhists . . . throughout Asia are solidly behind me' when he had a handful of adherents; the would-be Dr Evil who warned diplomats to heed his words 'before I press the button and inaugurate . . . a new period of bloodshed'. Wasserstein quotes Trebitsch at length and it is this voice – absurd, bombastic, petty and querulous – that echoes in the mind long after the book is closed. There is also a cruel comedy in the shape of Trebitsch's career. Each minor deception leads him into deeper and more dangerous waters. With its ever-escalating jeopardy his story has the relentless mechanics of farce (which, of course, are also those of tragedy).

There is comedy too in the way Wasserstein tells his story, with an eye for the ludicrous detail. Perhaps the most cherishable revelation is that Trebitsch owned an expensive set of bed linen, monogrammed with his initials, and allowed this to dictate his numerous pseudonyms. We can only imagine the groans from the Foreign Office as reports came in (yet again) that a Tibor Lehotzky, Theodor Lakatos, Thomas Lorincz or Leo Tandler was up to something murky in Central Europe . . .

Wasserstein's canniest move, however, is to play straight man to his own protagonist. No matter how bonkers it gets, Trebitsch's story is told as if it were a perfectly serious and quite conventional piece of history, underpinned at each point by scholarly citation. Only occasionally does the biographer forego his neutral tone and allow himself an exasperated aside – 'What, it may be asked, was the point of this nonsensical contretemps?'

As a historian, Wasserstein felt obliged to draw some sort of wider significance from his subject, and he did so by placing him in his times – an era of world crisis and collapsing empires that saw the rise of Lenin, Mussolini and Hitler. In this context, Trebitsch can be seen less as a one-off joke and more as a 'microcosm of global lunacy'. Anyone reading his story today will be uncomfortably struck by contemporary parallels. Had he been alive now, he would certainly have wreaked entertaining havoc in our 'post-truth' society of fake news and 'alternative facts'. We can all think of modern leaders who remind us of Trebitsch Lincoln. We may or may not find this funny.

JONATHAN LAW is a writer and editor living in Buckinghamshire. His latest book, *The Whartons of Winchendon*, tells the true story of one of the strangest families in English history, featuring incest, treason, fairies and the self-proclaimed Solar King of the World. People have found it quite funny.

Mr Gryce Meets His Match

KATE TYTE

Imagine you are at a pub quiz. It's the literature round and the theme is literary firsts. What was the first novel in English? What was the first detective story? Readers of *Slightly Foxed* could probably hazard a guess at *Robinson Crusoe* and *The Murders in the Rue Morgue*. But what was the first ever piece of detective fiction written by a woman? It's a question likely to leave most readers stumped. But just in case it ever comes up, the answer is *The Leavenworth Case* by Anna Katharine Green, published in 1878.

Green was born in 1846 in Brooklyn, New York. She graduated from Ripley Female College in Vermont and had ambitions to become a poet but, despite some early promise, never had much success with her verse. Undeterred, she changed direction and began work on a mystery novel. She wrote in secrecy for six years before showing the manuscript to her father, a lawyer whose experiences had partly inspired the story. *Leavenworth* was an instant sensation and sold over 750,000 copies within fifteen years of publication.

Leavenworth is narrated by the young lawyer of a rich business-man, Horatio Leavenworth, found murdered in his Fifth Avenue mansion. The investigation is led by Ebenezer Gryce of the NYPD. Gryce is more a shambolic Columbo than a dashing Sherlock Holmes – 'not the thin, wiry individual with the piercing eye you are doubt-less expecting to see . . . Mr Gryce was a portly, comfortable personage with an eye that never pierced, that did not even rest on

---

Anna Katharine Green, *That Affair Next Door* (1897), is out of print but we can obtain second-hand copies.

you.' *Leavenworth* introduced many of the elements of detective fiction that later came to be standard features: a Watson-like assistant-cum-narrator; plenty of evidence pointing towards a love interest; and a final trap set for the killer. It is tightly plotted, fast-paced and so realistic in its use of legal and police procedure that Yale Law School made it required reading. The novel also contains all the trappings of Victorian melodrama: secret weddings, mysterious disappearances, sinister letters, false identities, wrangling over an inheritance, stagey dialogue and lashings of sentimentality.

Anna Katharine Green wrote over forty novels, and her admirers ranged from Wilkie Collins to Arthur Conan Doyle who, on a trip to the States in 1894, was eager to meet her. Her eighth book to feature Ebenezer Gryce was *That Affair Next Door*, published in 1897. It introduces a new narrator and the first of Green's female sleuths, Miss Amelia Butterworth. Miss Butterworth is a spinster, a busybody and an obvious forerunner of Miss Marple.

Amelia Butterworth appears to have led a sedate life until the night of 17 September 1895, when she hears a carriage draw up at the adjoining house. 'I am not an inquisitive woman,' she begins, but 'I could not resist the temptation of leaving my bed and taking a peep through the curtains of my window.' She spies a young couple entering the residence of the Van Burnam family, and ten minutes later she sees the man leaving, alone. This is odd because the Van Burnams are on holiday and their house is empty. When the young woman fails to reappear the next day Butterworth becomes suspicious and calls a policeman. A cleaner opens the door for him and Butterworth dashes inside before he can shut the door.

They find the woman lying dead, crushed beneath a heavy cabinet. When Gryce arrives to begin the investigation, Miss Butterworth takes an immediate dislike to him. Gryce refers to her as 'this other woman': 'he meant *me*, Miss Butterworth, of Colonial ancestry and no inconsiderable importance in the social world'. A battle of wits ensues, with Miss Butterworth determined to prove her worth. When the dead woman's hat is discovered, she immediately points out that it has only been worn once, and when, subsequently, the coroner asks how she knows, she explains that it has only one small hole from a hatpin. Having satisfied herself that she is just as shrewd and observant as Gryce, Miss Butterworth begins her own amateur investigation, hoping to beat the detective at his own game and exonerate his main suspect. 'I was astonished to discover how much I was enjoying myself,' she says: 'though I have had no adventures, I feel capable of them.'

The plot of *That Affair* is satisfyingly convoluted, with many twists and turns, surprise revelations, false trails and red herrings. It centres on establishing the identity of the dead woman (crushed beyond recognition) and the man who entered the house with her. Was it the reckless younger brother, estranged from his family because he has married a pretty but lower-class girl, who is now missing? Or was it the elder brother, perhaps secretly having an affair with his sister-in-law? Or was it someone else altogether?

Miss Butterworth is a resourceful sleuth. She eavesdrops, observes, questions and bribes, tailing suspects, posing as a nurse so she can secretly search a room, and investigating insalubrious boarding-houses, hotels and laundries. And, possessed as she is of a sense of dignity and propriety, she forces her maid Lena to accompany her on many of these expeditions. Lena is more than happy to join in and proves surprisingly quick-thinking and capable.

Clothing and other subtle signifiers of status play a large part in unravelling *That Affair*'s tangled web of assumed and mistaken identities. In this respect Miss Butterworth's snobbery, her encyclopaedic knowledge of society gossip and her obsessive eye for the details of social niceties give her an edge over Gryce. Luckily for the modern reader, she clearly spells out the significance of the department store brands and millinery designs under discussion. The dead woman's identity, for example, is unknown but Miss Butterworth says she must be young because 'her narrow, pointed shoes show she has not yet reached the years of discretion'.

Miss Butterworth is a wonderful comic creation and a delightfully unreliable narrator. She is clever, observant, daring and indomitable in her quest for the truth. She is also deeply prejudiced, judgemental, snobbish, spiteful, mean-spirited, proud and, above all, nosy.

The battle-of-the-sexes element in the contest between Gryce's professional investigation and Butterworth's amateur one adds humour and tension to the proceedings. Their investigations follow completely different assumptions and uncover radically different (though equally pertinent) information. Miss Butterworth openly taunts Gryce and argues with him and these verbal duels make for the wittiest dialogue in the novel. Eventually, albeit grudgingly, Gryce comes to accept Miss Butterfield as more than a mere busybody. At the conclusion of the book, she in turn declares that 'Mr Gryce has never been quite the same man since the clearing up of this mystery,' and that if he had only listened to her . . . but then she checks herself and says, 'modest depreciation of myself [is] one of the chief attributes of my character'.

Miss Butterworth might have the last word, but during the course of the book she also becomes more likeable. She forges lifelong friendships, offers a home to an unfortunate woman, sees justice done and saves at least one lady from a bigamous marriage to a gold-digging imposter. So perhaps we can forgive her her many faults, allow her her moment of triumph and be grateful that she's not actually our next-door neighbour.

KATE TYTE lives in Portugal where she teaches and writes short stories, which have appeared in several magazines and podcasts. She enjoys eavesdropping and people-watching, but her Portuguese is not yet good enough to uncover any crimes.

Twice Upon a Time

ALASTAIR GLEGG

Starting a story with 'Once upon a time' does not guarantee a happy ending. In their classic collection of folk tales, the rather aptly named Brothers Grimm made sure there was a moral to every story: goodness is rewarded, evil is punished, sometimes quite brutally. Even Hans Christian Andersen's stories do not all end happily ever after: the prince who disguised himself as a swineherd to test the princess's devotion came to despise her and returned alone to his own little kingdom.

Many celebrated authors have tried their hand at fairy tales, with varying degrees of success. In 1888 Oscar Wilde wrote *Stories for Children* which included such classics as 'The Happy Prince', but they are really not intended for children. Instead of ending happily ever after they tend to close with an epigrammatic punchline, like the one that concludes 'The Devoted Friend':

> 'I told him a story with a moral' answered the linnet. 'Ah, that is always a very dangerous thing to do,' said the duck. And I quite agree with her.

Even his classic fable 'The Nightingale and the Rose' ends on a note intended not for children but perhaps for the members of Lady Windermere's fan club:

Oscar Wilde, *Stories for Children* (1888): O'Brien Press · Hb · 80pp · £13.99 · ISBN 9781847175892; T. H. White, *The Sword in the Stone* (1938): Collins · Pb · 368pp · £6.99 · ISBN 9780007263493. A. A. Milne's *Once on a Time* (1917) and James Thurber's *The 13 Clocks* (1950) are out of print, be we can obtain second-hand copies.

'What a silly thing love is,' said the student . . . 'I shall go back to Philosophy and Metaphysics.'

A. A. Milne recognized this difficulty in the introduction to his delightful *Once on a Time*, published in 1917:

> This is not a children's book. I do not mean by that . . . 'Not for children', which has an implication all its own . . . This is a fairy story for grown-ups.
>
> Children prefer incident to character; if character is to be drawn, it must be done broadly, in tar or whitewash. Read the old fairy stories, and you will see with what simplicity, with what perfection of method, the child's needs are met. Yet there must have been more in Fairyland than that . . . Princes were not all good or bad; fairy rings were not always helpful.
>
> Is it a children's book? Well, what do we mean by that? Is *The Wind in the Willows* a children's book? Is *Alice in Wonderland*? Is *Treasure Island*? These are masterpieces which we read with pleasure as children, but with how much more pleasure when we are grown-up.

In Milne's story, King Merriwig of Euralia is having breakfast with his charming daughter Princess Hyacinth when they are rudely disturbed by something passing over the castle, not just once but eighteen times. It is the King of neighbouring Barodia trying out his birthday present, a pair of seven-league boots, and displaying a lamentable lack of good manners which calls for the composition of a Stiff Note. King Merriwig is interrupted in this task by the beautiful but ambitious Countess Belvane, who has 'a passion for diary-keeping and the simpler forms of lyrical verse':

> Hail to thee blythe linnet,
> Bird thou clearly art,
> That from bush and in it
> Pourest thy full heart.

The chronicler acknowledges that 'many years after, another poet called Shelley plagiarized the idea, but handled it in a more artificial, and, to my way of thinking, decidedly inferior manner'.

Any fairy story with a princess must have a prince, and while her father is away at the inevitable war with Barodia, Hyacinth writes to Prince Udo of Araby, who might be able to advise her on affairs of state which are being taken over by the literary Countess. Unfortunately the Prince is bewitched on his way to Euralia, and arrives at the castle with the head and long ears of a rabbit, the mane and tail of a lion, and the mid-section of a woolly lamb: 'so undignified, so lacking in true pathos, and not even a whole rabbit'. Meals present a problem: they discover that he likes water-cress sandwiches, which seem to go with the ears, but don't suit the tail.

Prince Udo calls on the Princess Hyacinth and the Countess Belvane, by Susan Perl

The story is beautifully told: there are all sorts of subplots and complications before the essential but unusual happy ending, enlivened on occasion by the Countess's regrettable lapse into anapestic trimetres:

> Prince Udo, so dashing and bold
> Is apparently eighteen years old.
> It is eighteen years since
> This wonderful Prince
> Was born in the Palace, I'm told.

and her final diary entry: 'September 15th. Became good.' In Milne's own words: 'Read in it what you like; read it to whomever you like . . . either you will enjoy it or you won't. It is that sort of book.'

James Thurber is probably best known for *The Secret Life of Walter Mitty* and the articles and cartoons he produced for the *New Yorker*,

but he too ventured into the realm of fairy tales in 1950 with his fable
The 13 Clocks, which he created 'when he was supposed to be writing
something quite different, because he couldn't help himself'. It has
all the elements of the classic fairy tale but is full of Thurber's own
literary idiosyncrasies: his love of words, which he invents when there
aren't any that quite suit his purpose, his sometimes macabre sense of
humour, and his tendency to lapse into verse when a rhyme or allit-
eration distracts him. Ronald Searle's illustrations complement the
story – quirky and odd as usual, but perfect for this tale, studded as
it is with puns and sly allusions:

> Once upon a time in a gloomy castle on a lonely hill where
> there were thirteen clocks which would not go, there lived a
> cold aggressive Duke and his niece, the Princess Saralinda.

The Cold Duke and the Princess Saralinda, by Ronald Searle

The clocks had frozen on a snowy night ten years before and it is
always ten minutes to five in the castle: 'It's always Then. It's never
Now.' The Duke limps and cackles through the cold corridors, planning impossible new feats for the suitors of the beautiful Saralinda
who 'wore serenity brightly like a rainbow'. Many princes and other
suitors

came and tried and failed and disappeared and never came again. And some, as I have said, were slain for using names that start with X, or dropping spoons, or wearing rings, or speaking disrespectfully of sin.

The cold Duke is six feet four and 46 and even colder than he thinks he is. He has an invisible spy called Whisper, and is afraid of nothing except the Todal, which 'looks like a blob of glup . . . makes a sound like rabbits screaming, and smells of old unopened rooms'.

One day a wandering minstrel, quite properly 'a thing of shreds and patches', comes into town, courting the Princess and disaster with his songs:

> Hark, hark, the dogs do bark
> The Duke is fond of kittens.
> He likes to take their insides out,
> And use their fur as mittens.

The minstrel (who of course turns out to be a prince) is arrested and taken to the castle, where he is given an impossible task: to find a thousand gems in ninety-nine hours. If he fails the Duke will slit him from his guggle to his zatch and feed him to the geese. Fortunately he has some rather dubious help from the Gollux, who wears an indescribable hat and is somewhat unreliable, as he admits: 'I make mistakes, but I am on the side of good by accident and happenchance.'

They set off on their seemingly hopeless quest through an alliterative jungle of assonance where 'thorns grew thicker and thicker in a tricky thicket of bickering crickets' and many other trials, in order to find a maiden who once was known to weep jewels when she heard a truly tragic story. Alas, she is unmoved by the plight of the Prince and the sad tales of the Gollux, so something else must be attempted if he is not to discover the location of his guggle and his zatch the hard way.

Should we then conclude that there are two types of fairy stories, one for children and one for grown-ups? A difficult question, but T. H. White may have suggested an answer in *The Sword in the Stone* (1938). The Wart, who will grow up to be King Arthur,

> did not know what Merlin was talking about, but he liked him to talk. He did not like the grown-ups who talked down to him like a baby, but the ones who just went on talking in their usual way, leaving him to leap along in their wake, jumping at meanings, guessing, clutching at new words, and chuckling at complicated jokes as they suddenly dawned. He had the glee of the porpoise then, pouring and leaping through strange seas.

Perhaps one reason Milne's own stories have been favourites for so long is because he recognized this: surely Piglet's legendary uncle Trespassers W and Owl's Spotted or Herbaceous Backson are there not for the children, but for the grown-ups who take such pleasure in reading and rereading them the timeless tales.

ALASTAIR GLEGG lives on Vancouver Island and, like Molière's *bourgeois gentilhomme*, is delighted to learn that when he thinks he is just writing rude limericks he is actually composing anapestic trimetres.

94

Bibliography

Coming attractions

DAISY HAY goes walking with the Pallisers · MARTIN SORRELL travels to the end of the line · MARGARET DRABBLE follows the custom of the country · ANDREW JOYNES sails with Derek Walcott · SUZI FEAY is introduced to Hadrian the Seventh · JIM CRUMLEY treads in the footsteps of Neil Gunn · FRANCES DONNELLY discovers the real Lorin Jones